DOCUME

DIRECTING

AND

STORYTELLING

HOW TO DIRECT DOCUMENTARIES AND MORE!

JAMES R. MARTIN

J R MARTIN MEDIA INC / REAL DEAL PRESS
ORLANDO FLORIDA

Copyright © 2018, 2023 by James R. Martin. All rights reserved. No part of this publication may be reproduced, distributed or transmitted in any form or by any means, including photocopying, recording, or other electronic or mechanical methods, without the prior written permission of the author or publisher, except in the case of brief quotations embodied in critical reviews and certain other noncommercial uses permitted by copyright law. For permission requests, write to the publisher, addressed "Attention: Permissions Coordinator," at the address below.

J R Martin Media Inc/Real Deal Press
JR@jrmartinmedia.com
Publisher's Cataloging-in-Publication

Martin, James R.

Documentary Directing and Storytelling: How To Direct Documentaries and More / by James R. Martin -- 1st edition update.

p. cm.

Includes bibliographic references and index.
LCCN

ISBN-13: 978-1721679461

1. Documentary Films --Direction

2. Video Recording- Production and direction

3. Multimedia (Art)--Production and direction

4. .Storytelling   .I. Title.

Updated and edited-0306P -- ©2023

Trademarks

All terms mentioned in this book that are known to be trademarks or service marks have been appropriately capitalized. The author and the publisher can not attest to the accuracy of this information. Use of a term in this book should not be regarded as affecting the validity of any trademark or service mark.

Photographs and Illustrations

Unless otherwise noted and credited all photographs and illustrations are original copyrighted works of the author or public domain.

Fair Use Notice

This book may contain material the use of which has not always been specifically authorized by the copyright owner. Such material is being used in an effort to educationally advance understanding of environmental, political, human rights, economic, democratic, scientific, social justice and documentary issues etc. We believe this constitutes a "fair use" of any such copyrighted materials as proved for in section 107 of the US copyright law.

Warning and Disclaimer

Every effort has been made to make this book as complete and as accurate as possible, but no warranty or fitness is implied. The author and the publisher shall have neither liability, nor responsibility to any person or entity with respect to any loss or damage arising from the information contained in this book.

About The Author

James R. (Jim) Martin is an Emmy, award-winning Producer, Writer, and Director of Film, Television, Video, Multimedia, and Digital Media Productions. Formerly Director of the Documentary Filmmaking Course at Full Sail University in Winter Park, Florida, for 20 years. Professor Martin taught film production at Columbia College in Chicago for 13 years and Film Directing at the University of Central Florida.

Credits include two Emmy nominations and an Emmy Award for nationally aired PBS documentaries - Fired-up Public Housing is My Home and Chicago Film Festival, Golden Plaque, and Best Network Documentary, for Emmy nominated, and nationally aired, Wrapped In Steel. Editor, cameraman, producer, writer, and director of fiction and documentary films and videos.

Other Books by James R. Martin

Create Documentary Films, Videos and Multimedia 3rd Edition.
Actuality Interviewing and Listening.
Listen, Learn, Share.
Translator, writer, and editor English Edition,
Office and Home Tai Chi with Yue Zhang.
Translator, writer and editor, The Shaolin Temple Story,
with Hongyun Sun. Author Shi Yongxin.

Fiction
Silhouettes and Shadows, "Humanity Follows the Earth, *Earth Follows the Universe.*

Table Of Contents

Introduction ... 17

BASIC TYPES OF DOCUMENTARY AND NONFICTION ... 18

ACTUALITY DOCUMENTARY ... 18

DIRECT CINEMA AND CINÉMA VÉRITÉ ... 18

NONFICTION DOCUMENTARY ... 19

HYBRID DOCUMENTARIES ... 19

TELEVISION DOCUMENTARIES ... 19

"MOCKUMENTARY" ... 20

"ATTACK DOCUMENTARIES" ... 20

CHAPTER 1 ... 21

SO YOU WANT TO BE A DOCUMENTARY DIRECTOR?

FILMMAKER/DIRECTOR ... 25

JOB DESCRIPTION DIRECTOR ... 25

DIRECTING DOCUMENTARY PROJECTS ... 27

DESIGN AND VISION ... 27

Contemporary Documentary Filmmaking	28
Documentary and Nonfiction Media	30
Paintings or drawings	31
Animation and Montage	31
Oral history accounts	32
Interviews:	33
Audio:	33
First hand accounts	34
Home video, photograph albums	34
Newspapers, magazines, and public records	35
Literature	35
Mixed media	35
Nonfiction Presentations	35

Chapter 2 — 37

Documentary Storytelling — 37

Point of view (POV)	39
Rashomon Effect	43

SUBJECTIVE AND OBJECTIVE REALITY	44
SUBJECTIVITY AND DOCUMENTARY STORYTELLING	47
ACTUALITY STORYTELLING	49
TELLING A DOCUMENTARY STORY	51
STORYTELLING TOOLS	53
DOCUMENTARY GENRES	54
VISUAL ANTHROPOLOGY & ETHNOGRAPHIC DOCUMENTARIES	54
ARCHIVAL	57
DOCUMENTARY AS ART	58
GRAFFITI AS DOCUMENTARY ART	59
DOCUMENTARIES ABOUT THE ARTS	60
RELATIONSHIPS	63
MUSIC AND PERFORMANCE:	65
HUMANITIES AND SOCIAL SCIENCES	71
NATURE	75
NONFICTION EXPLORATIONS OF THE ENVIRONMENT AND OUR RELATIONSHIP WITH IT.	75
HUMAN INTEREST	79
SOCIAL ADVOCACY	80

Social and Political	82
Educational:	91
Mental Health	93
Public Service Sector	96
Family	97
Sports	97
Current or Topical Issues	98
Gender Issues	101
Religion	103
Personal Journeys	104
Media	108
Entertainment	109
Science	111
Training	113
Observer	115
Journalistic	117
Corporate	118
Public Relations	118

DOCUDRAMA	118
BASED ON A TRUE STORY	119
RECORDED EVENTS	120
HYBRID DOCUMENTARIES	120
HISTORICAL HYBRID DOCUMENTARIES	120
"MOCUMENTARY"	121
"ATTACKUMENTARY"	121
ACTUALITIES	122

CHAPTER 3 — 127

THE DIRECTOR AND PREPRODUCTION — 127

DEVELOPING/RESEARCHING DOCUMENTARY AND NONFICTION PROJECTS	127
IDEAS	127
PRE-VISUALIZATION	127
AUDIENCE	128
WHERE TO BEGIN RESEARCH	129
EXPLORING REALITY	130

FIND THE STORY	132
ASSESSING AN IDEA FOR A DOCUMENTARY FILM	132
CHECK LIST	132
CONSULTANTS	132
WRITING A CONCEPT AND TREATMENT	133
CONCEPT	133
TREATMENT	133
SHOOTING SCRIPT PREPARATION	134
WRITING THE SHOOTING SCRIPT	135
HOW TO FORMAT A MULTI COLUMN	
SHOOTING OR EDITING SCRIPT	139
FAIR USE	141
RULES OF THUMB TO CONSIDER	
BEFORE USING COPYRIGHTED MATERIAL.	142
WHAT IS FAIR USE OF COPYRIGHTED MATERIAL?	142
SHOOTING SCRIPT BREAKDOWN	145
CHOOSING A CREW	146

BASIC DOCUMENTARY FILM CREW

KEY JOB DESCRIPTIONS   147

WRITER   147

FIRST ASSISTANT DIRECTOR (AD)   147

SCRIPT SUPERVISOR   148

DIRECTOR OF PHOTOGRAPHY (DP)   148

GAFFER   148

CAMERA OPERATOR   149

SOUND MIXER   149

BOOM OPERATOR   149

EDITOR   150

PRODUCER   150

GRIPS   151

PRODUCTION ASSISTANTS (PA)   152

PREPRODUCTION CHECK LIST   152

COVERAGE   154

Chapter 4 — 155

The Director and Production — 155

Documentary Production — 159

Types of Scenes — 162

Action no Dialog — 162

Dialog no Action — 162

Action and Dialog — 163

Focal Length of Lens — 163

Framing and Point-of-View (POV) — 163

Shooting — 164

Coverage — 165

Shot Composition — 166

Lenses — 166

Shot Sizes — 168

Shot Angles — 171

EYE LINES IN INTERVIEW SITUATIONS	171
FILM ASPECT RATIOS	174
TELEVISION ASPECT RATIOS	174
LIGHTING CHOICES HELP TELL THE STORY	174
SHOOTING EXTERIORS WITH AVAILABLE LIGHT	174
LIGHTING INTERIOR LOCATIONS	175
WORKING WITH FLUORESCENT LIGHTS	176
WORKING IN LARGE SPACES	177
CAMERA MOVEMENT	180
CINEMATIC CONVENTIONS	181
MORE ON COVERAGE	183

CHAPTER 5 — 185

THE DIRECTOR AND POSTPRODUCTION — 185

EDITOR AND EDITING	186
REVIEWING COVERAGE	186
EDITING SCRIPT	187
ROUGH CUT	188

Fine Cut	188
Audio Tracks	189
Music	189
Effects	190
Post Production and Editing Basic Guide Lines	191
Transcripts	193
Test Screenings	193
Final Fine Cut	194
Audio Mix	195
Trailer	195
Production Stills and Video	196
Preview Screenings	196

On Line Resources and Documentary Reviews	198
Bibliography	199
Index	202

Where, When, and How to Begin

You are on a path right now, whatever age you might be, whatever place you find yourself. Every path has multiple crossroads of choices available to you all the time. It is never too soon or too late to change the direction of your way to your preferences.

This 2023 updated edition has been, edited, and additions and corrections made to increase readability. Please let us know about any editorial issues at jrmar2039@gmail.com
Thank you

Comments
at
http://www.jrmartinmedia.com/

jrmar2039@gmail.com

> "I think it's inevitable that people will come to find the documentary a more compelling and more important kind of film than fiction. Just as in literature, as the taste has moved from fiction to nonfiction, I think it's going to happen in film as well.
>
> In a way you're on a serendipitous journey, a journey which is much more akin to the life experience. When you see somebody on the screen in a documentary, you're really engaged with a person going through real life experiences.
>
> So for that period of time, as you watch the film, you are, in effect, in the shoes of another individual. What a privilege to have that experience."
>
> —Albert Maysles

Introduction

This book offers a learning experience and an exploration of directing documentary story projects. It provides fundamental and advanced ideas about actuality-style documentary filmmaking and nonfiction storytelling. Media include film, video, multimedia, and other resources. Finally, this book is excellent for anyone interested in documentary or nonfiction storytelling. There are numerous critical reviews of documentary films and the stories they tell from directing and filmmaking perspectives.

One of the best ways to learn about making successful documentary films is to watch mostly excellent documentaries guided by informed insight into how they were made. There are examples of documentaries included throughout the book, with information and specific criteria recommended for watching the documentary mentioned. I have made successful documentary films for over forty years while teaching film and documentary production at three universities in the US and other universities abroad for 36 years. It brings great joy that hundreds of my students have entered the film industry and become successful filmmakers in every aspect of the craft. Students produced many excellent documentaries in our classes over the years. This book shares my experience making films successfully and teaching others how to make documentaries. At the same time, much has been learned from the experience of working with talented professionals and students.

Knowledgeable directors understand the traditions and aesthetics of their work medium. They know the crafts involved and may have done some of those jobs themselves. This book focuses on directing and includes information experienced directors must understand about constructing a documentary story. What follows is practical information about directing documentaries, production theory, and other methods that can be applied to any genre in the actuality-style documentary and nonfiction realm.

Basic Types of Documentaries and Nonfiction

Documentaries are nonfiction, but all nonfiction is not a documentary. Here are a few brief definitions for a broad range of documentary categories that will be explored. Each documentary genre has sub-variations.

Actuality Documentary

It uses actual events, people, and stories, with no recreations or staged interviews. Narratives are developed that explore and document the human condition and connection with experienced reality.

Direct Cinema and Cinéma Vérité

Similar approaches were used in the U.S. and Europe beginning in the 1960s based on earlier notions about "truth" in cinema. The filmmakers generally record what is there in an observational posture. No interviews are conducted. The filmmakers adopt a "Fly on the wall" style of shooting. The story will take shape in the editing process.

Nonfiction documentary

Films for education, history, corporate, public relations, politics, and other areas use a mixture of action, recreations, actors, interviews (scripted and not scripted), archival materials, graphics, and animation to tell their stories by creating narrative structures.

Hybrid Documentaries

Hybrid documentaries are usually made for theatrical release or television, often featuring an on-camera host, who may be the filmmaker/director. Some hybrid documentaries may use actors or recreate scenes that happened in the past, using persons involved. Interviews, action, and archival materials may also be used. Hybrid documentaries combine different styles and may include art, animation, and graphics to help tell the story. Animated documentaries may be included in this category.

Television Documentaries

Television documentaries use an on-camera reporter or host who narrates and interviews subjects. Archival and live-action coverage are combined. These documentaries are usually topical and journalistic in content. Other television documentaries explore science, nature, and history using hybrid formats..

Reality TV is not a documentary or nonfiction. Reality TV is fiction. Individuals involved in the "reality story" may not be professional actors, but they do scripted actions in a scripted environment. They are directed, coached, and manipulated in said reality. The producers determine the outcomes in this format.

"Mockumentary"

As the name implies, these are satirical fictional, theatrical comedies, like Best In Show and This is Spinal Tap, using a faux documentary format. When done well, they are great entertainment but not documentaries or nonfiction.

"Attack Documentaries"

Films, videos, podcasts, and other formats are advertised as "documentaries" but are thinly disguised propaganda, personal attacks, and character assassination vehicles. These videos do not attempt to discuss issues or explore reality. Instead, they conjure up bogus conspiracy theories, unsubstantiated facts, and outright lies to "attack" a person, institution, policy, or politician. The goal is to cast doubt about an individual or institution. Stolen Honor was a character assassination attempt on Senator John Kerry, who was running for President of the United States. The film was fabricated using mock interviews and footage edited in a documentary style. Many attack documentary films are political and supported by political organizations with an ideology and political agenda. They go beyond ordinary propaganda in that they specialize in personal attacks.

Documentaries may be any length imaginable, from a few seconds to twenty-hour epics. A short documentary of any type is usually under thirty minutes. Feature-length documentaries are over sixty minutes, but more often around ninety minutes.

There are links highlighted throughout the book to examples and references.

Higligted subjects can be found at jrmartinmedia.com and support resources: https://jrmartinmedia.com/doc-book-blog/real-deal-press-book-products/publishing2/create-documentary-films/

Chapter 1

So You Want To Be A Documentary Director?

If you were to ask a classroom of new film students to raise their hands if they want to be a director, likely, at least half of the students in the class will quickly, and enthusiastically raise their hands. Very few of these students will end up working as directors in the real world. There are many reasons for this, circumstances, and demands that go beyond a mere talent for the vocation. It is also true that any of the students might evolve into the job of director at some point in their careers.

Often filmmakers and directors, who work in documentary production, have diverse backgrounds. A good number have studied film, after which they ultimately worked their way into directing. Others crossed over from related vocations or other non-related professions. Most share an interest in history, journalism, or social issues. Many have had an interest in photography or film from a young age. Very few people start as directors straight out of university, even though they may make some films independently and while studying.

Documentary filmmaker and director Ken Burns received an 8 mm film movie camera for his seventeenth birthday. He used the camera to shoot a documentary about an Ann Arbor factory. He then attended Hampshire College, an alternative school in Amherst, Massachusetts. Burns earned his Bachelor of Arts degree in film studies and design in 1975.

In 1976, in Walpole, New Hampshire, Burns, Elaine Mayes, Buddy Squires and college classmate Roger Sherman, opened *Florentine Films*. They worked together but also started doing other films under the Florentine Films Company name.

Burns worked freelance as a cinematographer for the BBC, Italian television, and others, and in 1977, having completed some documentary short films, he began work on adapting for film, David McCullough's book *The Great Bridge*, about the construction of the Brooklyn Bridge. The fifty-eight-minute, 1981 documentary, *Brooklyn Bridge*, was nominated for an Academy Award.

Ken Burns is an example of someone who had an interest in and love of history, a passion for photography, cinematography, and telling stories using film. After his now classic, nine-episode, ten-hour, documentary film *The Civil War*, he continued to direct documentaries as a filmmaker using a style, he developed based on using archival photographs, art, writing, film clips, and other materials to construct his narratives.

Frieda Lee Mock is an Academy Award®-winning filmmaker, director, producer, and writer who studied history and law, before graduating from UC Berkeley. She began her career in film at David Wolper Productions working on the National Geographic Jacques, Cousteau series. Her 1995 documentary film *Maya Lin: A Strong Clear Vision*, won an Academy Award for Best Documentary. She is also one of the founders of the American Film Foundation. Mock is an example of someone who got into documentary filmmaking from a non-related discipline.

Michael Moore is well known for his activist and hybrid journalistic style of documentary filmmaking. Moore came to film after working in the publishing world. After dropping out of the University of Michigan - Flint, he founded an alternative weekly magazine, The *Flint Voice* that ultimately became the *Michigan Voice*. Moore went on to become the editor of *Mother Jones Magazine* but was fired over disagreements with the publisher. Moore's first documentary film was *Roger & Me*. Moore went on to win the 2002 Feature Documentary, Academy Award for *Bowling For Columbine*. His documentaries since then, including *Fahrenheit 9/11*, and *Sicko* have been top-grossing films in the international theatrical market. Moore is not a film school graduate. He evolved to make documentaries from a personal and journalistic perspective.

Stacy Peralta came to fiction film and documentary from his career as a skateboarder. His first film was a fiction film in 1987 called *The Search for Animal Chin*. In 2001 he made the documentary *Dogtown and Z-Boys* which was very successful and lead to other successful documentary films like *Riding Giants* in 2004, then *Crips and Bloods* in 2008. Peralta graduated from Venice High School in California. He had no formal training in film before beginning his career in this area.

Spike Lee and Martin Scorsese are examples of fiction directors who crossover to nonfiction and make documentaries. Spike Lee with social documentaries like *4 Little Girls*, the *Katrina Documentary, When the Levees Broke,* and several others. Scorsese began, early on in his career, with *the Last Waltz* and later with *No Direction Home – Bob Dylan* and *Shine A Light – Rolling Stones* followed by *Fran Liebowitz – Public Speaking* in 2010. Spike Lee is an NYU Film School graduate who started his career with *She's Gotta Have It,* a fiction film, but now has many documentaries to his credit. Scorsese had a passion for making films as a child and earned an MFA in film directing from NYU in 1966.

Success for Scorsese as a director or filmmaker in the world of documentary and nonfiction appears to come from an ability to tell stories rather than being a film school graduate. Although film studies seems to be the key path to entering the film industry today. The next talent required is perseverance and the ability to survive the highly competitive world of making films. Graduating from a University with a degree in Film, BFA or MFA, does not guarantee you will make films or even get an entry-level job, let alone be a director. A good way to learn how to achieve your goal and survive in the film world is to read some biographies of various directors. Where they started and how they got to direct.

Finding financing and directing your short documentary film is one way of getting the experience and recognition required to find work directing. It's a way to learn and create a style you can showcase. Quite a few fiction directors started out making short documentaries before moving to fiction. Once again being a director requires the ability to tell a story, fiction or nonfiction using visual media.

FILMMAKER/DIRECTOR

Documentary directors are usually deeply involved in most aspects of the films they make. Some may shoot and edit as well as direct their films. They may write the shooting and/or editing script. Many produce as well as direct. While the term "filmmaker," in a general sense, may apply to any craft involved in the film production process, it has a special meaning when it comes to documentary films. It carries an auteur implication, meaning someone who does more than direct. It applies to "filmmakers" like Ken Burns, who are intimately involved in every aspect of the making of their documentaries It is difficult for anyone to make a feature-length documentary film by himself or herself. Most documentary directors are involved beyond the Directors Guild definition of "Director." They have a special style and commitment to actuality storytelling and exploring reality and truth.

JOB DESCRIPTION DIRECTOR

The director's role in making a documentary film varies depending on the type of nonfiction or documentary project. The director of a traditional documentary is usually the person doing the interviewing, working with the DP/camera operator, editor, and other key crew members.

The director is responsible for the look and feel of the project. If a producer is involved, they hire the director because they feel this is the right person to direct the production. Whether it's a traditional documentary or another nonfiction story, the director researches the concept of the documentary and comes up with a treatment and/or shooting script for the project. If it's not an actuality-based story, but instead a hybrid or nonfiction story using a documentary style, the director will take the script he or she is given and develop a look and feel to meet the script guidelines. At this point, as in fiction productions, the producer will sign off on what the director has decided to do.

The usual prerogatives and responsibilities of the director apply to the selection of certain key crew positions like the cinematographer and to staying within budget. Depending on the type of project, the director consults and works with the producer to develop a shooting schedule. The director works with the director of photography (DP) to plan compositions, camera moves, and lighting plots. The director scouts locations, often with the DP. In an actuality-based documentary, the director usually does the interviewing. During the editing process, the director works closely with the editor to choose usable footage, including stills and stock footage.

The writer in documentary production is often the director, and/or the producer. A writer may be brought in to work with the producer and/or director. There is usually a writer involved in a nonfiction production for an educational film, corporate training film, or television-style documentary production. Depending on the needs of the production the writer might be asked to work with the director to research and/or find archival and historical records for the development of a script for voice-over narration. Writers are also asked to work with the producer and director to maintain historical accuracy about events and narration.

Directing Documentary Projects

Documentary projects may require months or years to plan, fund, shoot, edit, and complete. If the project is something initiated by a filmmaker/director, he or she is involved throughout the process. Alternatively, a producer with a story idea may contact a director, early on, to see if they are interested in directing the film. In any event, there is usually a long-term involvement and commitment on the part of the director. Directors often have an interest in the subject and telling the story. Many directors specialize in certain categories of documentary films.

Design and Vision

A film director and a conductor of an orchestra have a lot in common. The documentary director has a treatment or shooting script instead of a score. The conductor has a vision of how the score should sound. A director must turn actions and words into images and sounds. The conductor leads the orchestra and is dependent on the ability and participation of each musician in the orchestra. If the third violinist doesn't play the right note, at the proper time the conductor's vision will be flawed. A film director leads the film crew, each of whom brings a special talent and skill to the project. The director needs to be able to motivate everyone on the crew to work as a team. Both the conductor and the director are creating something larger than the sum of its parts. One of the main functions of a film director is to have a vision for how to tell the story. Also, be able to involve all participants synergistically The director, like the orchestra conductor, facilitates many talented people to contribute their best effort.

In a documentary context, the director begins building a vision in preproduction. Since documentaries are an exploration of some actuality, research leads to a notion of where the story might go. The director pre-visualizes the many paths the story might take and brings those realities back to the editing room in the form of coverage. The coverage must be such that events, actions, and interviews can be woven into a story.

Contemporary Documentary Filmmaking

Documentary storytelling evolved through the 1920s, 30s, 40s, and 50s, based on the traditional cinematic and theatrical storytelling formats adapted to nonfiction. With the introduction of television, a new type of documentary evolved. In particular, the work of Fred Friendly and Edward R. Murrow typifies this approach. The documentaries employ a host, who is seen on camera, heard asking questions during interviews and doing voice-over narration. These programs included investigative documentaries. One example is a program that looked into the Senate hearings conducted by Senator Joseph McCarthy in the 1950's.

<u>Harvest of Shame,</u> [1] produced by David Lowe at CBS and narrated by Murrow was about migrant farm workers and was broadcast nationally in 1960 on Thanksgiving Day. It was prevented from being distributed beyond its television broadcast because of its depiction of a problem in the United States. This was censorship by corporations, probably influenced by government and political considerations.

At the same time during the nineteen sixties another type of documentary filmmaking emerged internationally. It may have been influenced by the work of early filmmakers like Dziga Vertov, based on the early Russian Film-Truth philosophy, "fragments of actuality assembled for meaningful impact." It was also connected with Lumière's concepts of simply capturing reality or "actuality" with no editing at all initially. In the United States, Direct Cinema grew out of the work of Robert Drew who called his style a

---

[1] Higligted subjects can be found at jrmartinmedia.com and support resources: https://jrmartinmedia.com/doc-book-blog/real-deal-press-book-products/publishing2/create-documentary-films/

form of "reporting" based on a photographic and journalistic approach. Drew worked for Life magazine, which featured photojournalism. This experience appears to have influenced his approach to film documentaries. Drew's documentary, *Primary*, is considered a "Direct Cinema" documentary related to the Cinéma vérité approach to "actuality cinema" or documentary filmmaking.

Drew's associate, D. A. Pennybacker, made, *Don't Look Back* which is another example of the Direct Cinema style of documentary filmmaking. Direct Cinema and Cinéma vérité were made possible by the development of portable, mostly six-teen millimeter film cameras and equipment. Direct Cinema and the Cinéma vérité style documentary, attempt to record people and events with as little interference as possible, and no direct interviews. The camera merely observes the subjects interacting and going about their lives. Events are therefore covered from an observational perspective. Modern, miniaturized, lightweight, and high-quality digital equipment make these styles of actuality documentary storytelling even more possible. The use of mobile phones to record events is a form of Cinéma vérité unless it is edited. One wonders what Lumière would have done with a modern mobile phone.

Some documentary filmmakers have a personal point of view on a subject. They set out to convey that view. Suppose they include factual information (accepted as having objective reality as a basis, which may or may not support their point of view). In that case, it creates a more balanced perspective regarding the issues involved. Their approach to telling the story will influence viewers to accept or not accept the subjective reality presented. Styles like Direct Cinema and Cinéma vérité, by default, offer a measure of authenticity that allows viewers to make their own decisions. However, neither Direct Cinema nor Cinéma vérité can claim to be completely objective. Any approach to storytelling by a human or their devices must be subjective. A point of view is established when a choice is made on how to tell the story.

Documentary and Nonfiction Media

Documentaries may be produced in many ways using one or more media. The criteria remain the same for all types of productions. Photographs may be used alone, in a book, exhibit, film, with or without audio, slide presentation, magazine, or newspaper. Titles, captions, and written or voiced comments may be used or not. A classic documentary book of photographs is Family of Man. The Family of Man was originally a photography exhibit curated by Edward Steichen, first shown in 1955 at the Museum of Modern Art in New York. According to Steichen, the exhibition represented the culmination of his career. The five-hundred and three photos were selected from almost two million pictures taken by two-hundred and seventy-three famous and unknown photographers in sixty-eight countries. They offer a unique snapshot of the human experience, which lingers on birth, love, and joy, but also touches on war, privation, illness, and death. He intended to visually prove the universality of the human experience and photography's role in its documentation..

The exhibit was turned into a book of the same name, containing an introduction by Carl Sandburg, Steichen's brother-in-law. The book was reproduced in various formats (most popularly a pocket-sized volume) in the late 1950s and reprinted in large format for its fortieth anniversary. It has sold more than four million copies. The exhibition later traveled in several versions to thirty-eight countries. More than nine million people viewed the exhibit. The only surviving presentation was awarded to Luxembourg, the land of Steichen's birth, and is displayed on permanent display in Clervaux. The museum is open to the public. In late 2022 Ken Burns authored *"Our America, A Photographic History"* which in many respects is a documentary-style book featuring an amazing collection of photographs from the past 183 years of American life. The book feels like it is in the same tradition as *"Family of Man,"* even though it has never been a museum exhibit.

PAINTINGS OR DRAWINGS

Art depicting events witnessed by the artist used in a film, video, or exhibited. Documentaries come in many forms. Usually, we think of film, video, or audio as documentary mediums. But an entire museum exhibit may be documentary in nature. The exhibition can use artwork, including photographs, graphics, and paintings. For example, a picture can be enlarged to the actual scale proportions of the building or object it depicts. It can then be used as part of a diorama. A diorama is a partially three-dimensional, full-size replica or scale model of an environment, typically showing historical events, nature scenes, or cityscapes for education purposes. An actuality-style documentary diorama recreates a cityscape using documentary photographs and other objects to recreate a street or location. Even graffiti, like the work of Bansky, has a documentary nature.

Painters like Edward Hopper created paintings depicting life and environments as the artist saw them then—their work documents life and environment in their style. The camera lens was the artist's eyes and talent. The paintings are not photographic in any way. But they subjectively render an actuality that existed at the time in the artist's view. Documentary filmmakers like Ken Burns and others use paintings in their documentary films to set the tone or provide a historical reference. There is an excellent short documentary titled Edward Hopper, narrated by Steve Martin, about Edward Hopper and his work. This documentary combines footage of places where Hopper lived, his work, interviews with Hopper and his wife, and others. It is a pleasure to watch an informative short educational documentary

ANIMATION AND MONTAGE

Sunrise in Tiananmen Square is a short (thirty-minute) autobiographical documentary that includes artwork, animation, photographs, newspaper clippings, audio effects, and narration. The documentary was made by Shui Bo Wang and was nominated for an Academy Award for Best Short Animated Film in 1998. The film is Wang's account of his life and experience in China during the 1960s, '70s, and '80s. It would be a mistake to characterize this documentary only as an "animated short film," which is not a typical film. Sunrise in Tiananmen Square incorporates some animation but should also be considered a cinematic montage of actuality-style materials, edited with audio effects, narration, music, and animated scenes. It certainly qualifies as a short documentary film. It is a fast-paced story of both historical and cultural significance. It is available on YouTube and the National Film Board of Canada (NFB.com)..

ORAL HISTORY ACCOUNTS

Documentaries are verbally presented, recorded, used alone, or in conjunction with photographs, and other documentation that supports the verbal account. Oral histories may also be recorded, transcribed, and included in a book. They are transcribed from actual interviews, with the subject, conducted by the writer or family members. Oral histories can be supplemented with journals, correspondence, and historic family documents They are also be presented as documentary-style audiobooks..

Studs Terkel (1912 to 2008) is an oral historian, author, and radio personality, who, for fifty years, traveled around America interviewing people from all walks of life. He talked to people about their jobs, war, and other subjects. His conversations with the famous and not famous became books and recordings that chronicled American history in the 20th Century. It is said that Terkel loved to talk, but one of his best talents was the ability to listen. He could do interviews with no written questions and be able to improvise on a theme that came up in a conversation. His books, using oral histories, were documentary in substance. "All of the books," Terkel said, "deal with the lives of ordinary people, not celebrities. What it's like to be a certain kind of person, at a certain circumstance, at a certain time." – NPR.org. A few oral history books by Studs Terkel are *Hard Times, The Good War, Working, Division Street America, Will The Circle Be Unbroken,* and *Hope Dies Last.*

INTERVIEWS

Interviews (Edited or not edited) on film, video, or audio recorders are usually transcribed, edited, and used in most actuality-style documentary projects. As stand-alone recordings, they might be used as a podcast or in a multimedia context, like an exhibit. An interview can also be used as a magazine, newspaper, blog, or website article. An actuality-style interview can be a spontaneous conversation with the subject conducted by the interviewer, director, or writer. As mentioned, Studs Terkel used transcribed interviews to create oral histories in his books.

A documentary interview may create a narrative along with the action.

Audio

Documentaries can be made using only audio resources. National Public Radio (NPR) in the United States does this style of documentary. Narration, interviews, music, and effects are used to produce the documentary. Audio-only documentaries may also be produced as podcasts or other means for use on the Internet. Documentaries can be made as audiobooks. .

First-hand accounts

Events recorded by individuals or groups may be documentaries. In this era of the "selfie," documentaries based on recorded first-person accounts are possible. There are many documentary-style short clips to be seen on social media sites. Many are unedited clips of an observed action, someone being silly, or pets in action. These clips are often edited together on some theme. But they are still archival in substance. Many fit a rough definition of "Direct Cinema" or Cinéma vérité documentaries. For the central part, the clips represent auteur observers and their point-of-view. This may be a "dash cam" clip of a traffic accident or an iPhone recording of some social or civil interaction. By definition, these and many other observer videos are archival in nature. However, you can use these clips in a documentary story. There are also many short (one to seven-minute) documentaries on social media sites. Three examples include YouTube, Facebook, and Tic Toc. These short documentaries come from individuals, charitable groups, political organizations, or other sources.

Home video and photograph albums

In addition to home video and photography, other forms of documentation are valuable for constructing a documentary story. Over the years, recordings of people and events have included painted family portraits and older methods of recording reality. Family biographies, profiles, and oral histories can all be built on these resources. Correspondence, documents, drawings, and other memorabilia may help to tell the story.

Newspapers, Magazines, and Public Records

Newspapers, magazines, articles, and public records are good sources of documentary material. They are archival resources that may be used to demonstrate or give examples mentioned in an interview. Whole stories may also be compiled from these resources to construct a compilation historical or biographical documentary. Archival materials including newspaper clippings, documents, artifacts, and objects provide depth and texture to a story.

Literature and Fiction Film

Nonfiction and fiction offer cultural and historical realities. A clip from a fiction film or a quote from a book can add depth to a story.

Mixed Media

Film and/or video productions using all or some of the preceding media can be used for multimedia documentary exhibits in museums or other venues.

Nonfiction Presentations

A documentary-style may be used for a Keynote® or Power Point® presentation and less formal types of reports. It is important to note that while there are many resources available for use in a documentary they may not be of high enough quality for professional applications.

Restrepo Outpost - Korengal Valley - Afghanistan

"The surrounding mountains rose to 10,000 feet; all traversed on foot. Long operations meant carrying enough camera batteries to last a week or more on top of the fifty pounds of gear required on even ordinary patrols. Cameras got smashed into rocks, clogged with dirt, and hit with shell cartridges during firefights."

Restrepo Filmmakers

Tim Heartherten and Sebastian Junger

Chapter 2

Documentary Storytelling

Documentary storytelling is as old as human life, cave paintings, and Neolithic nomads passing on hunting skills and survival stories. It is one of humanity's most important ways of passing on information and exploring reality. Early fiction and folklore are based on the human experience. Documenting what is seen and experienced is an attempt to understand and interpret the actuality that Homo sapiens face trying to survive in each generation.

Documentary stories were told orally when there was no written language. Someone who experiences being chased by a bear, and survives, passes on the tale from their point of view. To illustrate, they may have traced the route or location of the chase in the earth or drawn the bear on a cave wall. Now everyone knew what the bear looked like and where it might lurk. This story is passed down to the next generation, neighbors, and other families in the vicinity until it becomes a legend, embellished by each generation, no doubt. At this point, the story may be considered a fable or cultural icon.

In his documentary *Cave of Dreams*, Werner Herzog takes us inside Chauvet-Pont-d'Arc caves in Southern France, where impressive, thirty-two-thousand-year-old wall paintings document the animals these humans encountered. Older drawings and wall paintings exist in other locations around the world.

Herzog shot the documentary in 3D to capture the interior of the cave. In an interview with Documentary Filmmaker and BFA Professor Dr. Sun, Herzog said, "I only used 3D once in a cave, but it was a natural decision, and I didn't plan to do it in 3D. Because when I saw the cave paintings in photos, they looked like they were painted on pretty much flat walls. But once in the caves before [shooting], they're wildly undulating waves, recesses, and pillars. So, 3D seemed appropriate." -- Herzog, Beijing China, 2018

Documentaries explore reality in the hope of revealing some truth. To do this, they record or "document" actuality, which is happening now. Documentaries do not employ actors or stage events. Interviews are not rehearsed or coached. The information collected on film, video, still photography, or audio recording is edited into a story that the director feels represents the actuality they experienced and observed.

Generally, when documentary formats are employed, there is some latitude in presenting the subject matter and how the subject matter is defined. Nonfiction films and videos are found in the humanities and social sciences, corporate training, public relations, and sales projects. The big difference between them is in subjectivity and point of view.

The first motion pictures were called "actuality documentaries" made by the Lumière Brothers over one-hundred-thirty-five years ago. *Workers Leaving the Factory* and *Arrival of a Train* are each about one minute long. They have a single camera point of view and no editing. Louis Lumière strongly advocated only showing what he called "actuality." A documentary or nonfiction story explores actual events witnessed and recorded in some fashion. The documentary presents these actual events in a nonfiction story context. No staging actors or editing. Only recording, in some way, what is observed. A documentary does not employ actors to recreate reality. As soon as actors are used or a script is written detailing what will happen, even if it is based on a true story or event, it becomes a fictional recreation.

Nonfiction or documentary-style stories may use different media combined or alone to create a documentary story. For example, film or video, photographs, and audio, to make a film documentary. A slide presentation may also use a documentary format. An exhibit of photographs, like The Family of Man, is also a documentary. Documentaries may use audio alone to create a nonfiction story. Fine Art, graphics, and graffiti may also be documentary in nature.

In many ways, film or video documentaries are like visual nonfiction books. The stories they tell can be about a variety of different subjects. They may be informational, educational, entertaining, political, and on any topic found in the nonfiction area of a library or bookstore. Like a nonfiction book, documentary films make their POV known to viewers. Documentaries are subject to having their POV or premises accepted or disputed by the viewer. Just because they use actuality-style materials to present a view of reality on a given subject doesn't mean that the realities they depict are objective. A human point of view cannot help but be subjective.

Academy Award-nominated, feature documentary Restrepo, has a point of view that can't be ignored. The POV is subjective and from the inside looking out. *Restrepo* is a "bullets over your head, crawl on your belly" documentary experience in which you will "take fire" with combat soldiers fighting in the Korengal Valley near the Pakistan border in Afghanistan. Someone who hasn't been in a military combat situation cannot know what it's like. This documentary may be as close as you can get to being there. The story begins with young soldiers on a train hours before deployment. Although combat-ready, they do not entirely grasp what they are headed into for the next fifteen months. It's a rude awakening when they finally arrive near the firebase, and their vehicles come under fire from the Taliban. Even in the compound, walking around without drawing fire is impossible. There's at least one firefight every day. The result of these opening scenes gives the viewer a first-hand taste of what the soldiers are experiencing.

On an assignment to write for Vanity Fair, Sebastian Junger and Tim Hetherington visited and were embedded with the Second Platoon for one year. They shot 150 hours of footage in every situation, including going on patrol with the soldiers. The vérité footage is complemented by interviews with selected soldiers separately from the combat zone. On patrol one night, Hetherington fell and broke his fibula. He walked all night with his injury to not slow down the patrol. In Bagram, he had a metal plate put in, went back to the U.S., but decided to return to Afghanistan before fully recovered.

It took the filmmakers time to gain the soldiers' confidence. Tim Hetherington and Sebastian Junger made ten trips to the Kornengal Valley from 2007 to 2008.

According to the filmmakers: *"The surrounding mountains rose to 10,000 feet. All traversed on foot. Long operations meant carrying enough camera batteries to last a week or more on top of the fifty pounds of gear required on even ordinary patrols. Cameras got smashed into rocks, clogged with dirt, and hit with shell cartridges during firefights. Men were killed and wounded during filming, so there was a constant issue of when it was OK to turn on the cameras and when it was not. Only the filmmakers' close relationship with the platoon's men allowed them to keep filming in situations where other journalists might have been told to stop."*

Restrepo is a combination of documentary styles. The camera goes beyond a Direct Cinema or Cinéma vérité approach in that it also takes on the first-person point of view of a soldier in a combat environment. Interviews used in the film are lit and set against a black curtain, shot back at the Battalion Headquarters in Italy. They are in stark contrast to the war zone footage.

The uniqueness and success of Restrepo are that it creates an actuality from the soldier's point of view. The politics and other factors of their having to be there are not explored. It is the intimate story of soldiers in combat conditions, fighting daily with no breaks, living in the trenches. Restrepo goes beyond fictional wartime drama where the viewer suspends disbelief for ninety minutes to imagine what it might be like in combat. There is no need to "suspend disbelief" in this documentary. Restrepo is reminiscent of [The Anderson Platoon](), a 1967 documentary from the Vietnam era, where the filmmakers are also embedded with a combat platoon. Both films explore the soldiers' lives, the daily issues, how they deal with the constant threat of death for themselves and fellow warriors, and their willingness to continue fighting.

Michael Moore's documentary style begins with a point of view that is, without apology, his own. Michael Moore is a contemporary documentary filmmaker whose work appears to have been inspired, in part, by the tenants of John Grierson, who believed that the sole purpose of documentary films was advocacy. Grierson believed in relentless advocacy when it came to humanistic subjects. There is no "fairness" or feigned objectivity allowed.

A look around the world indicates some issues certainly meet the criteria of being social or ethical problems. When a documentary filmmaker like Michael Moore sees that many people in the United States lack adequate health care, he feels compelled to address this issue. This approach leads to a narrative that strongly advocates a cause. The trouble with the "advocacy, no holds barred" approach is that it often shows only one part of the story. Including both sides of a story is not necessarily an attempt to be objective or fair. It may support a point of view by allowing the viewer to examine issues and make an informed choice. It also takes the wind out of extremist opponents of the topic who argue that all the facts were not included and those who exaggerate minor issues.

In the documentary Sicko, Moore humorously shows how Americans have been conditioned to react negatively to anything even remotely connected with the word "socialism." For example, "socialized medicine." Specific reforms like Social Security, enacted by President Roosevelt (FDR) after the depression, helped Capitalism in the United States survive, possibly showing that there might be a best-of-both-worlds solution to the problem.

Most people will accept an advocacy documentary even if they disagree that there is a problem. They will consider any solutions proposed. What gets people riled up is when the documentary takes on a political point of view opposite to their own. Controversial subjects like government, war, social and ethnic equality, human rights, gender issues, and religion provoke emotional responses and lapses of reason.

Moore's documentary style begins with his participation as an on-camera investigative reporter. He narrates the documentary story, which may also include archival material and past action or interviews. He has a friendly appearance and interview style but is relentless in getting answers from people who don't always want to cooperate. Moore has a good sense of irony and humor that audiences appreciate. Cinematography and editing are professional in his documentaries.

Rashomon Effect
Rashomon is a 1950 Japanese fiction film directed by Akira Kurosawa, working closely with cinematographer Kazuo Miyagawa. It stars Toshiro Mifune, Machiko Kyo, and Masayuki Mori. It is fiction.

The film's narrative structure reflects the impossibility of obtaining the truth about an event because of conflicting witness accounts. Psychologists use the term "Rashomon Effect" to describe any situation in which the reality of an event is complicated to verify due to the conflicting reports of witnesses. Police are reminded of this phenomenon when trying to get eyewitness statements. The Rashomon Effect is essential to consider when directing a documentary film. It points to the subjective nature of what people may say or do in a documentary situation.

Subjective and Objective Reality

Philosophically there are numerous arguments about human subjectivity and objectivity, but what does it all mean to documentary and nonfiction storytellers? It is essential to discuss these issues because of the need to explore actuality and pass on what was observed. As documentary storytellers, we develop a point of view that attempts to find truth in those realities.

Not being aware of the subjective nature of the human mind or ignoring it facilitates creating fiction or propaganda. Propaganda distorts or skews reality, actuality, and fact to present a false alternative reality. Intentionally or unintentionally, it is possible to create stories that manipulate the viewer by allowing subjective filtering and manipulation of information to the point that the story becomes fictional.

Proponents of certain philosophical concepts contend that despite our subjective natures and realities, there is an "objective reality." The idea is that despite everything, there are facts that are true or false when examined. So that no matter how subjective our realities might be, these "objective realities" cannot be ignored. For example, if someone jumps in front of a speeding train, it is true that if it hits them, they will be killed despite any reality they may perceive. If someone lives at a specific address and states they live elsewhere, what they have claimed is factually not true, therefore, false. They have failed the test of objective reality. There is no gray area.

Philosophers, past and present, worldwide contend that all reality is subjective and that whatever is believed to be reality is reality. Therefore, there is no true or false, only what is perceived as true or false. In Buddhist philosophy, thoughts are impermanent and subject to passing priorities. There is "No Self," only random thoughts, feelings, and perceptions passing through the mind.

Modern psychologists, particularly evolutionary psychologists, theorize that human thought is based on two primary priorities: survival and procreation. The human mind will manipulate information, actions, or situations to serve these needs. In this modular view of the human mind, no self or decision-maker is in charge. Instead, a spokesperson, a public relations module, communicate subjective interpretations of reality to the person's consciousness and the outside world. In most cases, these modules manipulate information and experience to the benefit and needs of the mind and body it represents.

This indicates to the documentary director or filmmaker that all interpretations of reality from individuals must be considered subjective. One approach might be presenting multiple accounts of any reality or situation. Allow contradictory statements to surface in the face of actuality and objective reality. Documentary filmmakers and nonfiction storytellers dealing with issues that pertain to the human condition, social, political, and other critical areas need some standards, considerations, and ethics to guide them in their storytelling pursuits. The first step is understanding one's realities, biases, and cultural prerogatives. Observe these filters and be able to recognize them before reacting or forming an opinion.

Five (5) Broken Cameras, an Academy Award-nominated feature-length documentary, is an example of a story with a point of view that, while subjective, is honest in depicting the actuality in which the filmmaker finds himself living. In this documentary, the point of view is from residents living in the village of Bil'in on the West Bank. It explores the resident's non-violent protests and how the Israeli military and settlers react. *5 Broken Cameras* is a video recorded by Emad Burnet, a Palestinian farmer. The footage shot beginning in 2005 is given to Guy Davidi, an Israeli, who becomes co-director of the documentary. Davidi structures and edits the story.

Over five years, the Israeli military violently destroyed five of Emad's cameras. But each time, he gets a new camera and continues shooting Israeli settlements on land that was once his olive groves. This is the land of his family and neighbors. He films massive barriers built across the land and the military routing peaceful protesters. He records the injury and death of Palestinians who are protesting. The Israeli military seriously injures Emad himself as his young son stands by.

The story is partly built around the birth of Emad's son and what the son has grown up experiencing on the West Bank. It also represents five phases of Emad's life, paralleled with the five cameras getting broken. *5 Broken Cameras* is a first-person account of what has happened to the filmmaker, family, and friends on the West Bank over the past six years. This subjective, personal, inside view is never seen on the nightly news in Israel or other countries. Emad's perspective is from the inside looking out. You soon learn what it feels like to be a Palestinian living in the West Bank through the eyes of a farming family that, up until 2005, could take trips to the ocean and travel about freely. But a family now surrounded by fences, barriers, gates, and missing much of their land.

Guy Davidi, co-director and co-editor, brought story structure to the footage, basing it around what was shot with each camera until it was broken. The story begins with Emad purchasing a camera to document his son's birth. Emad starts to record the actuality around him with his olive groves confiscated.

This documentary is made possible by video cameras that anyone can own. *5 Broken Cameras* could not have been made without the advances in small portable video cameras that allowed everyone to document the life around them from a personal point of view. Technology continues to offer new ways to document life around us. Even our cell phones can be used for photography or recording video and audio.

Subjectivity and Documentary storytelling

Many journalists, documentary filmmakers, television pundits, and others believe they can be objective. They are either naïve, arrogant, or delusional. Even when dealing with facts determined to be true or false, objective reality is elusive. Humans are subjective in their thoughts and actions. From birth, each person becomes more subjective daily as they experience life and observe parents, family, culture, and environment. Humans are programmed to be subjective by natural selection priorities. Among other filters, two natural selection considerations are survival and procreation. However, many of these primal subjective survival filters are no longer necessary. For example, the filter that everyone who is not a member of our tribe, "the other," is less than human or threatening in some way. This filter runs deep in the human mind. The way to deal with tribalism is to be mindful of this hindrance when it appears. It is essential to recognize our subjective natures. The process of making documentaries requires the filmmaker to be aware of their subjective nature and its tendencies. Directing an actuality-style documentary requires adopting a viewpoint allowing the subject to tell their own story. This should result in a view from the inside looking out, which helps mitigate the filmmakers' subjectivity and external viewpoint.

Propaganda

What separates a documentary like *5 Broken Cameras* from propaganda is that the film does not pretend to be anything but this man's and his neighbor's subjective experience. Most documentary filmmakers do not get involved in making propaganda because it aims to manipulate others into believing a distorted point of view. A personal opinion is distorted to the point that it is fictional and directly related to what is called "spin" today. Propaganda often skews reality to promote one ideological, political, or religious view.

A group or organization may make an informational nonfiction film to "educate" individuals who are members of that group. It is internal propaganda. However, if it is used to promote that ideology to individuals outside the members of that group, it becomes Propaganda, with a capital "P" by definition. Propaganda is any "documentary" made by a government, political group, or religion for dissemination to the general public.

This definition of propaganda precluded two excellent documentary films sponsored by the U.S. Department of Agriculture from being shown in theaters in 1937. *The Plow That Broke The Plains* and *The River*, directed by Pare Lorenz, were withdrawn from theatrical distribution after congressional outcries that they were "New Deal," propaganda by the Franklin Roosevelt administration. By definition, they were propaganda, even though the stories they told were accurate and informative. Ideological and political groups have been known to promote intolerance, racial or religious hatred, and distorted realities of convincing others that their beliefs are the only realities. Fictional information based on false assumptions is presented as objective and righteous to persuade others that their way is the "true" and that an individual or group is somehow evil. Before and during World War II, German propaganda films are classic examples of depicting Jews, Roma, and other ethnic groups as evil and inferior to Germans

The Plow That Broke The Plains
A U.S. Documentary Film
by Pare Lorenz

The Plow That Broke The Plains

ACTUALITY-STYLE STORYTELLING

A documentary explores some aspect of human reality that is witnessed happening and recorded in some way. Actuality-style documentaries rely on non-invented situations and actions, i.e., actual events and spontaneous interviews with the subjects (not actors). How do the opinions of interviewed people compare with objective reality concepts? Can facts be found that confirm or contradict what has been said? Rather than using third-party, voice-over reporting, actuality documentaries mainly rely on first-person accounts to tell the story. In The *Civil War* documentary, Ken Burns uses historians to give perspective about letters written by people living at that time. A soldier writes a letter from the battlefield to his wife or family. The letter is equivalent to a first-person interview. Documents, artifacts, and other materials are all actuality sources.

"...We turn a blind eye to what surrounds us and a deaf ear to humanity's never-ending cry." – Night and Fog

Another style of actuality storytelling is demonstrated in *Night and Fog*, the 1955 French documentary by Alain Resnais. *Night and Fog* is incredibly cinematic, using montage editing to construct the story. This is not an easy documentary film to watch. The film graphically demonstrates the horror of the holocaust and the eleven million people who were murdered. There are no reenactments or speculations in this thirty-minute historical documentary essay. There is actuality, questions, and reflection about how and why something like this could happen and why it must never happen again in human history.

Night and Fog was made in 1955, ten years after World War II ended. It combines color footage shot in 1955 of the abandoned German concentration camps with captured German black-and-white film footage, and photographs, along with photos and footage shot by the Allies who liberated the camps. Music by Hannus Eisler accompanies the story with third-party narration by Jean Caroll. The result, some say, goes beyond traditional documentary filmmaking, creating a nonfiction essay on the film.

Since *Night and Fog* was made, many fictional films have been produced based on true stories or other information. Still, these films have yet to have the impact of *Night and Fog*, which methodically explores the actuality of this gruesome time in history using the context of the concentration camps. Night and Fog demonstrates an editing technique that pieces together a mirror of events and places, then and now, in a cuts-only montage. The color footage of the camps and the environment from 1955, in juxtaposition to the more abstract black-and-white archival/historical footage, moves you back in time. The actuality of that time and place becomes emotionally transparent. The approach Resnais uses in this documentary has influenced nonfiction filmmakers since it was made. It presents an objective reality about human actions that are difficult to comprehend. Yet similar events with names like "ethnic cleansing" still happen in different places worldwide today.

Telling a Documentary Story

Any story, whatever the medium, needs to have a beginning, middle, and end. It must also have a plot, drama, conflict, timing, and pacing. It requires a storyteller who knows how to communicate with their audience. There is no reason a documentary should be boring. In many instances, the filmmaker must find the story and present it in a way that engages the audience without distorting the actuality of the subject. This is a challenging task.

A documentary that skillfully takes advantage of conflict, drama, and timing to engage the audience is *Murder Ball*, directed by Henry Alex Rubin and Dana Adam Shapiro. It uses actuality footage, graphics, and excellent editing to present a reality that could have easily distorted the actuality. The film uses parallel editing of various characters and events to create a three-act dramatic structure based on actuality-style footage. Naturally occurring drama and conflict are employed in telling the story without distorting actual events. *Murder Ball* focuses on the USA Quadriplegic Rugby team's path to the 2004 Olympics in Greece, their rivalry with the Canadian team, its coach Joe Soares, and the US Quad Rugby players. The film's pace does not slacken as it takes you with these rugby warriors on their quest to win the Olympic Gold in Athens.

In the opening scenes, you quickly know several players through their words, actions, and interviews with their friends and families. The sport of wheelchair rugby is highly competitive, as are the participants. The rivalry between the USA and Canada is intensified by the animosity of the US team members toward Joe Soares, an ex-US player who has "defected" to become the coach of the Canadian team. This angst is intensified after the US team, undefeated in eleven years, lost a game to the Canadian team, coached by Soares, in Vancouver. After the game, one of the U.S. players asks Soares, "how it feels to be a traitor to his country?" One of the unique aspects of this documentary is that you are drawn into the players' lives and given an understanding of their disabilities in a non-condescending fashion. Instead, there is empathy and respect for these athletes who have overcome adversity and ask for no sympathy. This documentary is about a sport and athletes who have come a long way to play it.

Murder Ball is nonfiction but is a documentary structured like an action or dramatic fiction film scripted in three acts. Act One establishes characters, a back story, rivalry, and the U.S. as an underdog. The rivalry between the two teams, the US players versus Joe Soares and the Canadians, provides a clear protagonist and antagonist in Act Two. Joe Soares, himself wheelchair-bound, aggressive, and often insensitive behavior, makes him the person to dislike. However, toward the middle of the film, he gets some redeeming value when he attends his non-jock son's concert. Another, more subtle antagonist in the movie is the personal physical limitations the athletes must overcome to play this contact sport. Act three is the final confrontation and resolution of the rivalry. *Murder Ball* was nominated for an Oscar as Best Documentary Film and had an impressive list of awards, including one for editing. The prize for editing is well deserved since editing provided a structure for the story and kept an excellent balance between action and interviews throughout the film.

Storytelling Tools

Auguste and Louis Lumière's 1895 documentary, Arrival of a Train, tells its story in one minute. A platform of people, a train approaches and arrives. Passengers get off and on the train. This might not sound exciting or dramatic to a modern audience. However, it was surprising, even frightening, to audiences in 1895 who had never seen a motion picture film. More options and tools can be used to construct a documentary story today than in 1895. The more layers of subjective choices between the subject and the filmmaker, the further from actuality and the more opportunity for unintentional distortions. Directors and everyone involved in the process must endeavor to capture and mirror the reality they find. This is a challenging goal, as everything that the filmmakers do is subjective by default. For example, even basic choices, like selecting a camera lens, an angle, and the size of a shot, interpret the event. Each option must be considered for how it will present the event or subject. An interview with the cameraperson and the interviewer standing while the interviewee is sitting immediately results in a condescending point of view. A close-up of an individual or an object makes a different statement than a medium or long shot. The director must be aware of these choices and work to either neutralize the point of view as best possible or know why a particular option is being made. A skilled director can visually imagine how a scene will be edited based on the coverage they obtain.

Documentary Genres

Actuality-style documentaries can be divided into categories or genres, some of which take on specific requirements related to the subject or discipline for which they are intended. Most documentaries generally explore some aspect of the human condition or knowledge base. Fields may be in the humanities, arts, sciences, medicine, nature, culture, and other areas like travel, recreation, sports, economics, and journalistic investigation. Documentaries may cross over into more than one category.

Visual Anthropology and Ethnographic Documentaries

Two disciplines with particular guidelines for documentation are Visual Anthropology and Ethnographic documentaries. These guidelines are intended to preserve the actuality of events and the people they depict. Directors attempting to make documentaries in this area should either be involved in the disciplines or work with consultants to understand the requirements for these types of documentaries.

Visual Anthropology, a part of social anthropology, has grown to encompass a wide range of visual recordings, including performance, arts, visual arts, cultural, and human behavior. Ethnographic films look at the way of life of societies or ethnic groups. Some early ethnographic films preserved the history or culture of primitive peoples. However, they did not adhere to strict observer status. This type of documentary is sometimes called "salvage ethnography." There is quite a bit of discussion among Visual Anthropologists and Ethnographic filmmakers about how to record their subjects, not to taint them with outside influences.

By today's standards, Robert Flaherty's Nanook of the North is considered "salvage ethnography" or "ethnofiction." But Flaherty's goal for the first feature-length documentary was to preserve for posterity the way of life of the Inuit people he came to know and get his documentary into the theaters. For example, when filming in 1916 – 1920 (release 1922), the Inuit already used rifles for hunting. At the request of Nanook and Flaherty, only traditional hunting weapons were used in the film. The Inuit still knew how to hunt without rifles. Despite modern criticism, the documentary is the only visual representation of the Inuit people and their (pre-European invasion) lifestyle. In addition, Flaherty shot the documentary twice as his original footage was destroyed in a fire. He also trained Inuit people to work with him as crew members. He screened footage for the Inuit and got feedback from them.

Flaherty has been accused of staging scenes, picking certain Inuit persons to be in the film, and not showing European influences. (Although there is an early scene at the trading post where Nanook is shown a gramophone). These are all things that modern Ethnographic filmmakers would not do, or would they? Starting in the 1970's Judith and David MacDougall began subtitling their subjects' speaking and went on to make films that involved more collaborative relationships with their issues. With the availability of small video cameras, ethnographic filmmakers have given cameras to the subjects and allowed them to shoot their activities. Collaborating with a few anthropologists, Robert Gardner, a filmmaker, produced the documentary Dead Birds (1964). It studied ritual warfare among the Dani people of New Guinea. David Maybury Lewis used several cameras in his films to capture multiple simultaneous points of view.

These attempts to capture the documented subjects' "objective" point of view are commendable. We must do the best we can. However, it seems impossible to film or record people's customs and culture without influencing the result and changing the actuality. The camera itself changes reality. To test this idea, pick up any camera or cell phone and ask someone if you can take their picture. They will assume a pose of some kind for the photo. This result tells its own story in some respects, but it is not the actuality that existed before the camera was introduced and permission was requested. Suppose the cameraperson becomes invisible and moves around taking photographs or shooting video undetected by the subjects. While this would remove one layer of subjectivity, it would still be the subjective view of the cameraperson, his camera, lens, angle, and recording media. Also, a director asks for certain types of shots and coverage. By following specific guidelines, Visual Anthropologists and Ethnographic documentary filmmakers work to minimize personal priorities and the impact of cameras and crew on the subjects they are recording. One approach might be to adopt a point of view and film with that as the documentary's goal. For example, a documentary about marriage customs in a specific ethnic group could focus on the point of view of the parents of the bride and groom. Tell the story from their perspective.

While not an ethnographic documentary, Meet The Patels, using a hybrid documentary and fiction format, explores the pressure on Indian American families to maintain their culture and traditions, focusing on marriage. The point of view is from assimilated second-generation children. Humorously, many issues typical to immigrant families of this and other ethnic groups are examined. The main character in the documentary, Ravi V Patel, experiences many traditions unique to the "Patel Clan," one of the largest ethnic groups in India. Ravi and his sister Geeta codirect the documentary. Both are second-generation American Patels. This is reminiscent of the ethnographic filmmakers giving the cameras to the subjects.

Archival

Setting up several cameras in neutral positions and using drones to record an event or interaction between people can be done for archival purposes. There would be no editing. The footage is reviewed and stored away for posterity. For example, if the above setup were used to cover a large outdoor music concert, it would remain archival footage until it was edited to become a documentary. Footage and photographs shot non-professionally by families and others are also considered archival. Other archival sources are documents, paintings, and artifacts. Once archival footage is given to sources and subjectively edited. It is no longer archival.

Documentary as Art

Actuality-style documentary film footage, photographs, and audio material are used artistically to produce the vision of the filmmaker/artist. An early example of this idea was *Berlin Symphony of a Great City,* made in 1927 by Walther Rutman. It depicted Berlin from dawn to dusk, emphasizing the city's light, rhythms, and patterns. A symphonic score was composed for the documentary and performed with it at screenings. The actuality footage in black and white produced an abstract vision of Berlin when the film was shot. The film was made for artistic rather than documentary purposes. Even so, the documentary nature of the effort preserves the actuality of Berlin at this time.

In a modern context, one internationally known filmmaker, who makes documentaries and fiction feature films, believes his work goes beyond the labels attached to fiction and nonfiction. Werner Herzog often categorizes his documentaries as "theatrical feature films, wearing a documentary mask." He feels he is a poet, creating narratives exploring reality. He believes facts and objectivity are illusions. He admits to casting his characters, rehearsing scenes, staging, and using commentary and music to create his visual poetry. He believes he has an "artistic license" when he tells his stories. He considers that more truth can be discovered beyond facts, which he compares to names in a phone book. In an interview at Beijing Film Academy, in Beijing, China, in March 2018, Herzog told Professor Sun:

"It's much more fluid, and as I said, many of my documentaries are not real documentaries. They have the mask, a feature film with a [documentary] mask. I think I should not make anyone nervous about making "documentaries." I say it in quotes, and I [also] make feature films."

Graffiti as Documentary Art

A good case can be made for considering certain types of Graffiti as documentary art. For example, graffiti by Bansky and others, seen on walls worldwide, artistically documents the environment and human activities. Exit Through the Gift Shop, a documentary film, takes a candid look at this subject and explores the Art World at the same time. Exit Through The Gift Shop incorporates several approaches. The footage that Thierry, the original shooter, contributes is old-school Direct Cinema, as "fly-on-the-wall" as it can be. Once Banksy gets involved, there is a Cinéma vérité activist approach, combined with interviews, music, and a third-party narrator.

Exit Through The Gift Shop, directed by Street Artist Banksy, begins with Thierry Guetta, a Frenchman living in LA who runs a trendy clothing shop. Thierry carries a camcorder everywhere he goes and compulsively shoots whatever interests him. After visiting his family in France, Thierry discovers that his cousin, living in France, is a graffiti artist known as the Enforcer. His cousin knows Shepard Fairey, a well-established Los Angeles Street artist. When Thierry returns from France, he contacts Fairey, who agrees to let Thierry go with him while he works. Thierry tells Shepard he's making a documentary about graffiti and street art. But Thierry has no idea how to make a documentary; he's just into recording events, which is almost everything he sees that interests him. He has hundreds of tapes sitting in storage boxes.

After seeing a ninety-minute cut of Thierry's attempt to make a documentary out of his random footage, Banksy suggests to Thierry that maybe he should go home and try doing some street art himself. Banksy claims he never dreamt that Thierry would decide to become a street artist commercially. As in all documentary efforts, you must wonder how much the filmmakers facilitated the story through their presence. How much did Banksy enable Thierry to recreate himself as a Street Artist? This is something one may never know. As a documentary filmmaker, you go where the story takes you. In any event, Banksy took over directing a new documentary.

Exit Through The Gift Shop is well worth spending some time watching. It's an independent documentary with a story to tell. It is sociological and anthropological to some extent. The documentary is edited and paced well, an entertaining night out with street artists. And when the dawn comes up, an illuminated glimpse into the contemporary commercial art world. A look at what the Graffiti and Street Art movement has become. In many respects, Banksy is holding up a mirror to himself, other street artists, and the art world regarding the commercialization of art and artists.

Documentaries about the Arts

Beautiful Losers begins with archival footage shot as early as the 1980s. It tells the story of outsiders who came together and found common ground in a small New York City storefront gallery. These are people with diverse backgrounds, including subcultures like skateboarding, hip-hop, surf, graffiti, and punk, who began to invent their art. With no real training, they established pop culture trends based on their self-taught art backgrounds. Today many of these non-traditional artists have become mainstream in the Pop Culture area. They are sought after for various types of projects, including art exhibits and by advertising agencies. Shepard Fairey, Ed Templeton, Harmony Korine, Mike Mills, Barry McGee, Chris Johanson, Geoff McFetridge, Jo Jackson, Magaret Kilgallen, Stephe Powers, and Thomas Campbell are names you may or may not recognize. However, their work is unmistakable in style and content.

This documentary is unique because the artists seen in *Beautiful Losers* became filmmakers and documented themselves along the way. Aaron Rose uses that archival footage and interviews to create a history of the artists, their progress, ultimate notoriety, and success. *Beautiful Losers* is a linear journey, sometimes slowing down the engrossing and informative film. *Beautiful Losers* could be more cinematic in its storytelling approach. There is no real sense of beginning and middle, although it does build up in the last minutes to an inspirational end. This is not to say that what is presented isn't interesting and valuable. There is a pattern of talking heads illustrated with archival "B" roll footage that feels redundant in what it says about the process these artists went through. What the documentary lacks very much is action. In some respects, it feels like it was edited to fit a ninety-minute time frame.

The editing in *Beautiful Losers* is a mundane mix of interviews, archival footage taken over the years of varying quality, and "B" roll. Beautiful Losers is essentially a compilation documentary building on archival footage. The footage does give you a feel for what it was like for them to come together in the eighties, but it does slow down the film. In some cases, the archival footage speaks for itself, but there is so much of it that the pace stops engaging. The interviews are good, and the artists involved project their personalities, views, and ideas. The interviews combined with seeing the work is the best quality of this documentary.

Art & Copy, directed by Doug Pray, might sound like a documentary about the history of advertising or how to create excellent advertising campaigns. But that would only be a small part of this superb documentary film. *Art & Copy* communicates on many levels. Its primary focus is on the creative process, the artists and craft people working in the industry, and how advertising fits into today's world. *Art & Copy* inspires anyone in the arts, film, and advertising.

Director Doug Pray constructs a story that begins with simple images, a man working for a billboard company, just like his father and grandfather have done. Statistics show how many advertising messages Americans are subject to each day. There is so much advertising today that most people feel inundated by the volume.

Many people try to ignore the onslaught as much as possible, but ignoring the messages on our phones and coming to us through emails and television is difficult.

Art & Copy includes interviews with people who, over the years, have created advertising that has been innovative and convincing. Their motivation and work are strong themes in this documentary. The names of industry legends like Lee Clow, Hal Riney, George Lois, Mary Wells, Jeff Goodby, Rich Silverstein, Phy K. Robinson, Dan Wieden, and David Kennedy may be different from household names. Still, their work, in many ways, has changed the way much of the world eats, plays, shops, works, and communicates. *Art & Copy* brings these people and their work together in a way that explores many issues surrounding the advertising industry. At the same time, the documentary presents a flowing visual commentary that provides the viewer with a context that transcends the words and glimpses of the advertising that has had such a strong influence on life in America and much of the world. The interviewees talked about their feelings regarding work, personal philosophy, individual occupations, and the creative process involved in advertising. It becomes clear that good advertising is good storytelling.

From a filmmaking standpoint, *Art & Copy* director Doug Pray creates a nonfiction visual story that goes beyond a basic documentary format without hybrid style compromises. Pray's work, starting with short documentary profiles sponsored by Doc Marten Shoes, shows an ability to focus on the subject and tell a story in a few minutes. The profiles were screened at the Silver Doc Film Festival. They included a portrait of a "Roadie" for a well-known band doing his job and a Dispatcher (motorcycle messenger) in London, among other documentaries.

In the documentary Scratch, Pray covers the art of "DJ'ing" with excellent footage and editing. The documentary compares the act of DJ'ing, using turntables, recordings, and technical devices, to creating music with a new instrument. His work shows innovation within the broad genre of documentary film storytelling. Art & Copy uses action, interviews, archival video, photographs, "B" roll, and music to tell the story. The documentary is entertaining and informative. It is a story anyone can enjoy and learn something simultaneously

RELATIONSHIPS

Cutie And The Boxer is a moving and thought-provoking journey into the lives of two artists in a relationship that has evolved over forty years. The story begins with the eightieth birthday of Ushio Shinohara. He and his wife, Norika, celebrate this event by lighting a candle on a small cake. Ushio and Norika are both artists, married now for forty years. There's about a twenty-year age difference between the two. They met when she was an art student who had just arrived in NYC from Japan. Norika has lived in Ushio's shadow for their entire relationship and is now struggling to find her identity. Until recently, she largely neglected her work to support Ushio and raise a son. She harbors some justifiable resentment, manifesting in her pushiness and controlling their domestic life. But even with all the stress and issues, these two people have an unmistakable bond.

The documentary's title, *Cutie And The Boxer*, is connected to one of Ushio's painting techniques: putting on boxing gloves, dipping them in paint, and punching the canvas from left to right. He still does this at age eighty and does sculptures and other paintings. Norika paints and draws. The first act of this documentary sets up the relationship between these two artists. They don't have much money and live mainly by selling Ushio's work. In the second act, there is more about the relationship over the years and the birth of their son. The third act sees several themes and issues resolved.

Cutie And The Boxer, directed by Zachary Heinzerling, introduces Ushio and Norika Shinohara in the opening scenes in a way that graphically shows one aspect of their relationship. It focuses on Ushio's work, with Norika supporting and assisting him in some cases. But it soon becomes clear that she's having some problems and issues she is discovering and wants to resolve. Ushio comments after one scene that "she didn't want to help him."

The first evidence of Norika's frustration comes when she is found working on some drawings, with captions narrated by a character Norika draws named Cutie. Cutie tells the story of "me and my husband, Bullie." She begins with drawings depicting her coming to NYC at nineteen years old and meeting Bullie, who was forty-one. She's impressed with him and soon falls in love. But the story reveals facts that don't always cast Bullie in a positive light. These drawings are combined with home video footage of the couple as time passes. There is also a clip, narrated by Edwin Neuman, a short biography of Ushio Shinohara coming from Japan to NYC in the 1970s. Shinohara was a well-known artist in Japan when he came to New York. In 1971 he fell in with other non-traditional artists like Andy Warhol.

Another aspect of the story is age. At eighty, Shinohara is still working. His drinking days are over due to health concerns. At sixty, Norika finds herself as an artist and woman. This story reflects how each of them deals with reality over time. What might seem like a negative comment is something else. Accepting the other person and their good and bad points are reflected in the daily banter of the couple. There is a story behind each remark. By the documentary's end, you have gained insight into this type of long-term relationship. The original *Cutie And The Boxer* score by Yasuaki Shimizu are perfect for the film. The cinematography and editing are excellent.

MUSIC AND PERFORMANCE:

Recording a musical concert for broadcast or archival purposes does not make it a documentary. However, most television coverage includes a director calling shots from each camera to be broadcast. Using multiple cameras to record a musical performance by an individual or a rock group is essentially archival. While the events have been "documented," they only become a documentary when they are explored beyond recording the performance.

A classic example of a documentary based on a concert made in 1978 is *The Last Waltz*, directed by Martin Scorsese. Best known for "Taxi Driver" at this point in his career, Scorsese first approached the project as more of an archival event about a concert. As he got into it, he realized there was a story here beyond the last show of a popular musical group. Scorsese asked about working on *The Last Waltz*, said, "it was a joy, it was a celebration, it was extraordinary inspiration listening to this music." To many, there will never be another band like *"THE BAND!"*

The Last Waltz is one of the best concert or musical documentaries ever. It became a musical documentary when it went beyond simply recording the concert. *The Last Waltz* transcends the concert event category by inter-cutting interviews with the band members about their experiences and why, after "sixteen years on the road," Robbie Robertson feels "it's an impossible way of life." The interview segments are skillfully blended with the performance footage to show how these musicians got to this point in their careers. In dramatic terms, it provides the backstory to *The Last Waltz* documentary.

One of the highlights of the film is the guest appearances of well-known musicians and singers, including Ronnie Hawkins, DR. John, Neil Young, The Staples, Neil Diamond, Joni Mitchell, Paul Butterfield, Muddy Waters, Erik Clapton, Emmylou Harris, Van Morrison, Bob Dylan, Ringo Starr, and Ron Wood of the Rolling Stones. Of course, everyone looked much younger than they would today! The Last Waltz is beautifully lit and shot. Credit for the lighting and cinematography goes to several people. Director of Photography and Camera Operators included Vilmos Zsigmon, Laslo Kovacs, David Myers, Bobby Byrne, Michale Watkins, Hiro Narita, also Camera Operators Fred Schuler, Joe Marquette, Ray J. DelaMtte, and Sean Doyle. Laslo Kovacs saves the day in one scene by shooting and covering Muddy Waters's performance while everyone else accidentally goes on break. David Myers used a handheld camera on the stage and was responsible for some great close-ups during the performances. Hiro Narita operated on a jib or track, getting higher angles.

The subjective layer of sets and lighting adds the filmmaker's point of view to the documentary. It provides a setting and helps to interpret the event. Scorsese did not tell the performers what to play or how to work. He shot the concert as it happened. He did elaborate preproduction planning about how he and his crew would cover the performances based on what numbers The Band said they would be performing. This pre-production planning is essential even for unpredictable events.

Scorsese did a multi-column shooting script with a storyboard and camera plot diagrams included so that all the camera operators would know what to shoot. In addition to the concert hall venue, Scorsese shot several extra numbers on a sound stage after the event. In these, he used a crane to get a different perspective and feel of the music and performers. The lighting felt like it was done to complement the Winterland venue concert hall lighting. The line between fiction and actuality is often a gray one. Scorsese's introduction of set and subjective lighting doesn't add a fictional aspect to the documentary. It simply enhances the environment where the concert's actuality occurs, helping to illuminate the subject.

It Might Get Loud, directed by Davis Guggenheim, tells the story of three well-known electric guitarists, each a legend in his own right. The Edge (U2), Jimmy Page (Led Zeppelin), and Jack White (The White Stripes, The Raconteurs) jam on an empty stage, beginning a dialog that covers more than their music. Each of these men has a unique style and approach. However, they all share a passion for the electric guitar and the music they produce with it. What ultimately emerges from the audio speakers when each of these musicians performs is their unique voices.

There's a lot to like in this well-paced journey that explores the passion these musicians feel for their music and where their love of music got started. There is archival footage of Jack White playing with bloody fingers, Jimmy Page reliving the first time he heard Rumble performed by Link Wray, and Edge playing Bloody

Sunday. What makes watching special is that you know what inspires their performances. This film's blend of past, present and sincere emotion creates the narrative.

It Might Get Loud is centered on a jam session that brings the three guitarists together. However, a large part of the story is about how they each got there and where they are now. The back story for each musician is parallel edited with live performances, interviews, and archival footage. The archival footage of performances by each musician provides an insightful dimension to where each person has been in their life and of their playing styles. From a technical perspective, *It Might Get Loud* uses parallel story development to contrast each of the three musicians, the music they play, their experience, and their unique passion for their craft. The extensive use of archival footage edited into segments along with interviews is integrated with short clips of the current jam session until the end of the film, where a more extended session ensues as a finale.

Gimme Shelter brings together the documentation of a concert tour and the direct cinema work of the Maysles Brothers. The 1970 film documents a Rolling Stones Concert tour beginning in New York City and ending with a free concert at the Altamonte Speedway near San Francisco, California. Three hundred thousand fans attend the concert. *Gimme Shelter* does not have any interviews. Typical of a Direct Cinema documentary, we are brought into the story as observers. In this case, we are more than "flies on the wall." It feels somehow that we, too, are in danger at times. This documentary is a fine example of the work of David Maysles, Albert Maysles, and Charlotte Zwerin, the same team that made other great documentaries, including Salesman in 1968. Salesman goes door-to-door with Bible Salesmen. Viewers of the documentary sit in as the salesmen pitch prospective customers and go to sales meetings and the local diner. The filmmakers in Maysles brothers and Direct Cinema documentary films seem invisible.

Gimme Shelter started as a concert tour documentary, but only a few pure performance scenes from the tour were used in the final film. More attention is paid to the upcoming concert in California. Events created a story no one anticipated. It is a story that came together in the editing room. Still, the scenes with Mick Jagger and the Rolling Stones performing reveal what the band was like then.

The documentary begins with New York concert footage. Then it takes us to a film editing room where Mick Jagger and the filmmakers watch film clips of the Altamonte Concert playing on a flatbed editing machine. The footage shows events unfolding, leading to a man being killed. After allegedly being disarmed of a pistol, this man is stabbed and beaten to death by a group of Hell's Angels in front of the stage. The murder is shot from the stage as the Rolling Stones perform "Under My Thumb." It's difficult to tell exactly what's happening until the footage is viewed frame-by-frame. There were, in total, four deaths and three births at the concert that day.

Early in the film, there are scenes of the Rolling Stones performing at tour venues, including Madison Square Garden, where relative calm prevails. While watching the promoters arrange to bring the concert to the Altamonte Speedway, it becomes clear that disaster may be looming. At the concert venue, long lines of cars are seen coming to the concert, along with people getting stoned, running around naked, and hanging out. The musicians performing before the Rolling Stones have difficulty keeping the stage clear, and a Hell's Angel hits one musician. When Mick Jagger and the Rolling Stones started performing "Sympathy for the Devil," the crowd became an unruly mob.

The filmmakers keep their cameras rolling and capture a tragic end to the concert. The documentary was created after filming ended, based on the catastrophic events at the Altamonte Speedway. The filmmakers used footage they shot previous to Altamonte to create foreshadowing of problems with things like the enormous crowds anticipated at the free concert.

Humanities and Social Sciences

Documentaries that explore issues and realities in the Humanities (Philosophy, Literature, Religion, Art, Music, History, Language) and the Social Sciences (Anthropology, Archaeology, Criminology, Demography, Economics, Human Geography, History, International Relations, and Political Science).

The National Endowment for the Humanities (NEH) and local humanities councils fund documentaries in all the above categories. Along with Columbia College Chicago, they supported <u>Wrapped In Steel,</u> a feature-length documentary directed by James R. Martin, author of this book. Wrapped In Steel is part of the four-year Southeast Chicago Community History project funded by NEH and the Illinois Humanities Council. Support of the local council was necessary to apply for a grant from NEH. Columbia College Chicago sponsored and supported the entire project, including the documentary film. The community history project is the dream of Michael Alexandroff, President of Columbia College, at this time.

The *Wrapped In Steel* documentary aims to help preserve the four neighborhood histories and reflect community experience to the residents, along with the current status of this multicultural, multi-ethnic community of one hundred thousand people. Many residents work in the steel industry or are recently laid off. After one year of research, while the community history project proceeds, filming begins and continues for another two years. Several parallel themes are identified. Themes include the workplace, family, ethnicity, religion, and politics. Photographs are collected from residents, cataloged, copied with permission, and returned. With permission, copies of the pictures are given to the local historical society. Filming covered events and interviews with residents, business leaders, scholars, and others. As time passes, a storyline is conceived that looks at the neighborhood along the previously mentioned parallel themes. The finished two-hour documentary is previewed for residents of the area. A ninety-minute version ran nationally on Public Television (PBS), was nominated for an Emmy, and received other awards, including "Best Documentary" at the Chicago Film Festival.

Historical Documentation is based on photographs, film, and other resources to visually represent that history falls under the humanities and social sciences. Documentaries often explore aspects of several disciplines simultaneously. Documentary film series about historical events, like *The Civil War*, by Ken Burns, or about important individuals socially or historically, fit into this category. Burns uses photographs, documents, archival film footage, interviews with subjects, experts, and actuality media to tell the story in his documentaries. The Civil War is primarily based on Civil War photographs and letters from persons involved, read by voice-over narrators. Burns uses camera moves over the pictures and sound effects to bring movement and action to the documentary.

Jazz is a nineteen-hour documentary series directed and produced by Ken Burns that is relevant historically and culturally. Jazz is one of Ken Burns' best documentary films. Like most of his work, the series transcends being solely a factual historical record. Burns puts the facts into a historical, musical, and social context. Jazz, the documentary, fits the evolution of Jazz music with American culture, Black History, people, and politics of the United States. The history of Jazz, it turns out, is born out of circumstances uniquely American, and to a large extent, in New Orleans in the 1890s.

"It is a creation of the African-American community there but incorporates all kinds of music heard in the streets of what was the country's most cosmopolitan city." Jazz

Jazz music soon moved out of New Orleans and became a national passion. This documentary will introduce you to Jazz or increase your appreciation and enjoyment of this music. The story begins by introducing the day's environment, politics, and culture, then explores how it got that way. Individual artists are highlighted against the backdrop of their time and place in the world. There are dozens of parallel themes that weave their way through this documentary. One theme in other documentaries, like Civil War and Baseball by Burns, is the ongoing, vitriolic backdrop of race relations and racism in America. The documentary does not ignore racial segregation and how black musicians were treated in America.

Another theme is the history of the country and the world, to some extent. The central theme, of course, is exploring jazz music, although some critics feel the documentary isn't inclusive enough of all who contributed. Despite this possibility, Jazz does a great job introducing those interested in music to the subject and whetting appetites for more. Documentary films are visual and always subject to holding the viewers' attention. Books can be read at any pace. Unlike a history book, with unlimited length and verbose explanations, a documentary film must be succinct, keep pace and fit into a time frame from which most people will view it. Music historians, experts, and professors would do well to consider this as a documentary film intended for all audiences, not a history book. Even nineteen hours is not enough to cover the history of Jazz completely.

Film and video are primarily visual mediums. More recently, sound has become an equal partner in storytelling in film and video. But documentary films are still dominated by the visible part of the presentation. A contemporary viewer/listener can see and hear simultaneously, absorb, understand, and appreciate the visual/audio gestalt. As tempting as it might be, filmmakers do not have the luxury in a documentary about music to hold a picture or a blank frame for the music to play for three minutes so that the composition can be listened to exclusively.

Ken Burns said, "Meaning accrues in duration." So, take your time, enjoy, and learn. When Ken Burns said, "meaning accrues in duration," he initially referred to an editing style that usually takes time. In the case of Jazz, the editing pace is driven by the music (four-hundred-ninety-seven individual pieces of music), which makes things feel like they are moving faster. There are times when it does seem the theme is digressing a bit too much into the context side of the story of Jazz, but not very often. Jazz both entertains and informs on many levels. The documentary offers a beautiful combination of music and story. In the words of Ken Burns, "[Jazz] is the soundtrack of America."

Ken Burns reflecting on his work in The Making of Jazz, a special short documentary on the first episode DVD, mentions that he has spent sixteen years working on three films: Civil War, Baseball, and Jazz. He repeats a quote by Gerald Early,

"When they study our civilization, two thousand years from now, there will only be three things that Americans will be known for: the Constitution, Baseball, and Jazz music. They're the three most beautiful things Americans have ever created." Gerald Early in Jazz

Burns goes on to say

> "...And JAZZ is also a story about race and race relations and prejudice, about minstrelsy and Jim Crow, lynchings and civil rights. JAZZ explores the uniquely American paradox that our greatest art form was created by those who have had the peculiar experience of being unfree in our supposedly free land. African Americans in general, and black jazz musicians in particular, carry a complicated message to the rest of us, a genetic memory of our great promise and our great failing, and the music they created and then generously shared with the rest of the world negotiates and reconciles the contradictions many of us would rather ignore. Embedded in the music, in its riveting biographies and soaring artistic achievement, can be found our oft-neglected conscience, a message of hope and transcendence, of affirmation in the face of adversity, unequaled in the unfolding drama and parade we call American history." -- Ken Burns

Nature: Nonfiction explorations of the environment and our relationship with it.

Does the man or woman in the street believe Global Warming exists? How do human activities in the environment affect civilization and the lives of all the other creatures with whom they share the planet? These productions may be seen on National Geographic, Discovery Channel, and other venues that make and air documentary-style nonfiction programs.

Academy Award-winning, *An Inconvenient Truth* (2006), directed by Davis Guggenheim, is a documentary that looks at the issue of Global Warming. It states its point of view and then looks at the reasons and facts that support this premise in the tradition of nonfiction writing and advocacy documentaries. The format of the documentary is based on a slide presentation that Vice President Al Gore presents in the documentary. There are also interviews with scientific experts and evidence given to support the premise that the planet is getting warmer. While this film is about the environment, it is also an advocacy documentary. It establishes its point of view clearly and presents an argument with scientific evidence that leads to the conclusion that there is global warming, to which human activity contributes. Guggenheim also directed documentaries, including *It Might Get Loud* and *Waiting For Superman*.

Blackfish, directed by Gabriela Cowperthwaite, is an advocacy documentary that falls into the treatment of animals and nature advocacy category. The filmmakers have issues with how Orca whales are treated in captivity. Specific critical points regarding the morality of caging animals may apply to all sea and land animals in captivity. But the final decision on this issue of how these intelligent sea mammals are treated is left for the viewer to decide. In the end, solutions to the problems are offered, like establishing sea sanctuaries for the captured whales where they can at least have some space to swim.

Blackfish is well-directed and edited. It was shot using a Canon 5D DSLR, according to INDB. Made in 2013, the eighty-three-minute documentary is fast-paced, using interviews, news foot-age, eyewitness coverage, and archival material. Another exciting documentary in this area is *The Cove*. The Cove is a documentary examining the capture and slaughter of dolphins in Japan. Many captured dolphins are sold to Sea World and other parks internationally. *The Cove* documentary, like *Blackfish*, makes it clear that these mammals are creatures that should not be hunted and kept in captivity to amuse humans. In this sense, both *Black Fish* and *The Cove* are advocacy documentaries.

Nominated for an Oscar in the Best Feature Length Documentary category, *Virunga*, a Netflix documentary, is a story that takes the viewer into the chaos of the war-torn Eastern Congo and the Virunga National Park, where dedicated Park Rangers struggle to protect the last of the Mountain Gorillas and preserve the park and its residents. There are several parallel themes in the story. One of the themes involves three young, orphaned gorillas rescued by the Park Rangers and still in their care. Caring for the young gorillas becomes increasingly difficult as the war encroaches on the park. Seeing these young gorillas and their affection for the Rangers is heartwarming.

The animals and humans in and around Virunga face similar problems as the war engulfs their constant struggle for survival. This documentary does an excellent job of telling the story by being there in the park. As events progress, the filmmakers travel with the rangers, the oil company (SOHO) security, indigenous people living there, government soldiers, and the rebels. The documentary shows the refugee camps on the southern border of Virunga Park, where thousands of people live, displaced by the rebels and war. Interviews and conversations with certain characters are conducted without the interviewees knowing it. This is a risky tactic for the filmmakers if caught since the value of a person's life appears low in the Eastern Congo.

Virunga combines nature documentary and journalistic reporting from a war zone. The filmmakers face many life-threatening situations as they go with Park Rangers through the park to check on the gorillas and other animals. The rangers must deal with poachers and rebel militias. The parallel development of multiple viewpoints helps explore the conflict and its human concerns.

Dogs Decoded, Nova/PBS documentary, fits the mold of being educational in content and purpose. How did dogs get to be our best friends? What do they know or understand? The documentary film *Dogs Decoded* sheds some light on those and other questions. It will surprise you in many ways. *Dogs Decoded* is directed by Dan Child. PBS categorizes it as a "Nature" documentary. However, it goes beyond the nature label in an educational context exploring how humans interact with an animal that has helped humans survive over thousands of years. The Nova series programs are educational television documentaries that include science.

One of the first things *Dogs Decoded* looks at is where dogs come from. Are they the domesticated descendants of wolves? Are they separate species? Research into dog DNA helps resolve these questions. In light of this new evidence, the documentary explores the relationship between humans and dogs going back thousands of years. *Dogs Decoded* connects the dots in science's search to find out more about how dogs evolved while being around humans. Do dogs understand human language? Do they acquire a vocabulary that allows us to communicate with them? Do they communicate with humans? *Dogs Decoded* answers these and many other questions. In one sequence, you will meet a dog that will amaze you with its ability to understand human language.

The structure of this documentary combines interviews with scientists, experts, and dog owners, along with action coverage of dogs that demonstrate what is being "decoded." Throughout, it explores the scientific and emotional attachment between humans and dogs.

Human Interest

Stories about how humans live, the environment, unique people, and other issues of interest. These documentaries take on aspects of different categories of documentary work by combining various themes. *Jiro Dreams of Sushi*, 2012, directed by David Gelb, is a documentary that communicates on several levels. *Jiro Dreams of Sushi* begins as the story of an eighty-five-year-old master sushi chef who creatively makes and serves sushi in his ten-seat sushi bar restaurant. Sukiyabashi Jiro is located in a Tokyo subway station. But this story has several themes that immediately surface and go beyond the act of making sushi, the art of which is beautifully shot in mouth-watering close-ups, accompanied by an original score by Philip Glass.

The documentary opens with an introduction to the restaurant and archival photographs of Jiro Ono, who was told to leave home at nine. He gets a job as an apprentice in a sushi restaurant. Early in the film, he discusses "picking an occupation you fall in love with. "You have to love your job. Once you learn the craft, your talent takes you to the next level." Jiro's words go beyond the art of making sushi and his basic approach to life. The documentary also offers insight into Japanese culture. *Jiro Dreams of Sushi* explores Jiro's relationship with his two sons, who have worked with him, starting as apprentices. The eldest son, Yoshikazu, seems caught in the shadow of his father, who is not ready to retire. Jiro, speaking about himself, does not feel he has reached perfection yet. Yoshikazu believes his duty as the eldest son is to stay with his father and continue his tradition. The second son is helped by the father to leave the family business and start a new restaurant. All of these themes are woven into the story.

Social Advocacy

John Grierson, the father of modern Social Advocacy Documentary Films, began with <u>Drifters</u> (1929), then films like *Coal Face* (1936) about the problems of coal miners in Great Britain, and then *Housing Problems* (1935). All of these films called for the need for social and political reform. He was unapologetic about his point of view. He believed that

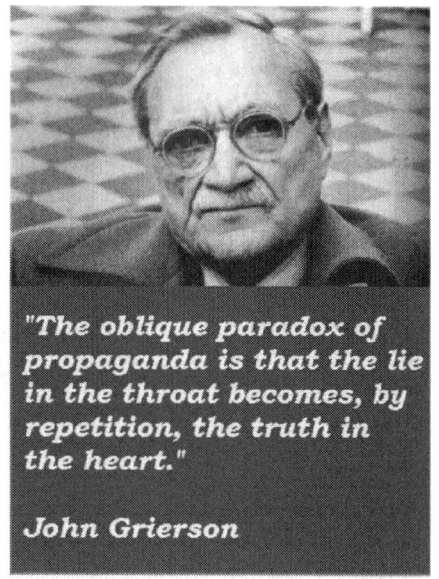

> "The oblique paradox of propaganda is that the lie in the throat becomes, by repetition, the truth in the heart."
>
> *John Grierson*

documentaries are a tool to point out problems and solve social issues. Grierson said, "I look on film as a pulpit."

Today social advocacy documentary topics include people living below the poverty line, human rights, the workplace, ethnicity, racism, issues regarding the human condition, gender equality, and exploration of social and political conditions. Ecological concerns may also cross over to social advocacy documentaries.

One of the great things about making documentaries is that it is always a learning experience. In Academy Award Winning, documentary <u>Born Into Brothels,</u> 2004, director Zana Briski, shares her firsthand experience making the film. She takes the viewer into the brothels of Kolkata, formerly known as Calcutta, in West Bengal, India. A city of 4.5 million people in an even larger metropolitan area of 15.7 million inhabitants and the capital of East India. Born Into Brothels takes place in the Red-Light district of Kolkata (Calcutta), where Zana Briski, a photographer from New York, initially embedded herself to document the life of the women who work there photographically. But she soon becomes more concerned with the children of the prostitutes. Children who are "Born Into Brothels." Because the women work in illegal trade, they are considered criminals, and their children are also branded as criminals. The girls will ultimately have no choice but to enter the sex trade (known locally as "the line"), and the boys will become involved in illegal activities like drug dealing.

Zana obtains cameras and gives them to some of the children. She teaches them to take pictures and see through the lens. The children become interested in the process and begin to create photographs that are first-hand portraits of the life they see around them. As Zana gets to know the children, she becomes dedicated to getting them out of the brothels and into a better life. Mainly the film focuses on eight or nine of the children. As the documentary progresses, the question arises as to whether "Art" can or will be permitted to transform the lives of the children.

Born Into Brothels combines first-person narration by Zana Briski, interviews with the children and mothers, and views of the environment. Montages using photographs taken by the children involved in the film are also used. You can see the children's progress taking pictures, and a glimmer of hope enters some of their lives. Each child has their own story that they tell as the film progresses. The cinematography is intimate, bringing you into the children's and their families world. Shooting is difficult in the available light-only environment. The editing of the documentary is excellent, keeping pace with the sounds and music of the story. Born Into Brothels is an essential documentary in many ways. It points out problems, explores issues, searches for solutions, and documents a process that positively alters the participants' reality. It also changes the perspective of the viewer of the film. Many documentaries point out problems, social issues, or historical concerns. Only a few documentaries inspire and facilitate change. *Born Into Brothels* is an exceptional documentary. Zana Briski shares her learning experience and the world being explored, as it happens, from start to finish. Born Into Brothels presents a model for using the creative process and learning photography to evoke change. It is a successful social advocacy documentary.

Social and Political
Social and political documentaries usually have a strong point of view that the filmmakers try to explain and champion.

Academy Award Winner Best Documentary 1976, *Harlan County USA*, directed by Barbara Kopple, is a solid social advocacy documentary built on actuality footage shot by the filmmakers as events unfolded. Harlan County, USA, begins in the mine with the coal miners, their work, and the environment in which they work. Dark, damp, dusty, cold, cramped spaces underground where an accident can cost everyone their lives. The camera goes with the miners as they are taken into the mine lying down on a conveyor belt, the roof of the shaft inches from their heads. You are with the miners as they crawl through tunnels and mine the coal. The processed coal makes its way on another conveyor belt to the surface and the light long before the miners, who will spend their day in the shadows. When the coal miners at Brookside voted to join the United Mine Workers (UMW), the Duke Power Company, owners of the mine, refused to accept the contract with the union, so the workers went on strike. Duke Power Company then attempts to bust the union and intimidate the workers violently. This was not the first-time workers rebelled against the coal mine owners. There are scenes in the documentary using archival footage that show previous strikes from the 1930s and some of the area's history.

Harlan County Director

This documentary tells the story of the coal miners and their families at a critical juncture in the history of Harlan County, Kentucky. People striking for better wages and working conditions is essential. One unique aspect of this story is the miners' wives, who decide to take an active role in the process. In this Kentucky version of "women's liberation," the women don't burn their bras. Instead, one woman, Lois Scott, uses her bra to carry a gun. Since any restrictions on the number of picketers apply to the workers, she and other women start working the picket line to support their husbands and the strike. The film crew is on the picket line with the strikers one night. They are attacked by a group of thugs led by Collins, hired by the coal company. They are out to beat the film crew and hurt or possibly kill Kopple, who is the focus of the attack. The filmmakers fight back, but the coal miner's wives come to the rescue. Part of the attack is filmed. The filmmakers manage to get a warrant for Collins's arrest.

The sheriff, in one scene of the film, serves the subpoena. Making this documentary required being on location for many months. The documentary style combines action, interviews, and Cinéma vérité activism. This is not the nightly news with some false notion of objectivity. The documentary has a humanistic perspective. The plight of these Americans, living in third-world conditions and being denied their constitutional rights by the mining company, is undoubtedly a cause worth advocating.

Because the filmmakers identify with the miners and are drawn into the story, the filmmakers, to some extent, become a catalyst to what happens during the strike. The mining company and others are intimidated by the fact that their activities and the attacks on the miners are being filmed. In some ways, the workers and their families may have felt enabled by the film crew there on location and empathetic to the miner's problems. The filmmakers allow the viewer to see into the lives of the miners, their families, and Harlan County. To do this, Kopple gained the miners and their family's confidence. There are scenes of strikers and state police confronting each other and meetings of strong women supporting the strikers in the film. Harlan County USA is a must-see documentary for anyone interested in making documentaries or learning about the history of America.

4 Little Girls takes the viewer back to 1963 and Birmingham, Alabama, amid the Civil Rights Movement struggles. It includes a look at the earlier history of Birmingham. The documentary revolves around four young girls killed on September 15, 1963, when a bomb went off at the Sixteenth Street Baptist Church in Birmingham. Joan Baez sings Richard Farina's Birmingham Sunday as archival photographs of the girls, their graves, and shots of troubled Birmingham stream by. Directed by Spike Lee, *4 Little Girls* extensively uses archival footage showing the deeply rooted racism prevalent in Birmingham in those days. The film uses archival photographs of the extended families of the four girls, as parents and others are interviewed. *4 Little Girls* is a documentary film that brings to life an episode in American History that needs to be shown to each new generation.

Spike Lee depicts what Birmingham is like for African Americans living there. Birmingham in the 1960s is racially segregated in every possible way. The documentary shows there is an active Klan organization with a large number of members on the police force. Homes and churches are frequently bombed while the police pretend they do not know who is doing it. It's crucial to understand Birmingham and Alabama in the 1960s. The church bombing is one of a long line of atrocities committed by certain racist elements living there. The state Governor, George

Wallace, not only turned a "blind eye" to the problems but also vowed to stop any form of integration. He is famous for standing in the doorway of the University of Alabama to block the first black student from entering.

4 Little Girls, beautifully edited by Sam Pollard, introduces each girl and her family. Denice McNair, Carol Robertson, Cynthia Wesley, and Addie May Collins were the girls killed that Sunday. The interviews with their parents, siblings, and friends are intercut with photographs showing who these girls are and establishing them as real people, not just pictures in a newspaper. The sound design, including Joan Baez singing Birmingham Sunday over the opening scenes, other music, and sound effects help tell the story.

4 Little Girls combines life in Birmingham and the coming of the civil rights movement to the city. Martin Luther King is jailed for demonstrating in Birmingham. The Southern Christian Leadership Conference (SCLC) organizes students, leads protests, and "sit-ins" at lunch counters. The actuality in Birmingham, presented in *4 Little Girls*, is supported by witnesses, archival footage, photographs, and newspaper clips. For many years, Birmingham's toxic atmosphere enabled and harbored the men who committed this heinous act on September 15, 1963. There are interviews with Rev. James Bevel, Rev Wyatt Tee Walker, Ossie Davis, Rev Jessie Jackson, Walter Cronkite, Andrew Young, and even George W. Wallace, who mutters away about giving textbooks to Black students and having a Black friend. This Black friend is his male nurse, whom Wallace repeatedly asks to join him in the shot.

4 Little Girls is a documentary that can't be ignored. It brings to light not only the tragic murder of the four young girls but also the terrible results of racism and the persecution of humans by other humans. *4 Little Girls* makes it clear that the impact of all bigotry, racism and religious intolerance leads to disaster for all concerned. Viewing this documentary today or any time in the future is a reminder of what hate produces.

Spike Lee has created a definitive work that examines the issues and questions around the tragic death of the 4 Little Girls. He has done this in a traditional documentary fashion, passing all the tests for actuality and objective reality. The film documents a tragedy, but *4 Little Girls* is not intended to stir old wounds. It seems to stand as a reminder that the destructive mindset of hate and bigotry can raise its ugly head again to be used against any group of people.

Many documentaries with social or political themes advocate specific ideas while exploring a subject. Films like Michael Moore's *Fahrenheit 911* and *Why We Fight* by Eugene Jarecki examine social and political issues, how people feel about government, politics, war, states' rights, and the constitution. Topical issues from any area of the political spectrum also fall under this category.

Academy Award-winning, *Inside Job*, 2010, directed by Charles Ferguson, looks at the Global international crisis of 2008 and the events leading up to it. The documentary goes beyond recording the events historically and socially. It discusses the cause of the catastrophe and names the culprits who cashed in, benefitting at the taxpayers' expense. Inside Job is the rare documentary that definitively looks at problems, issues, causes, and outcomes and then offers solutions to stop them from happening again.

Inside Job combines archival material, interviews, narration by Matt Damon, and footage that supports the discussions and complements the story. What could have been one hundred and nine minutes of talking heads becomes a well-paced, visually exciting documentary. The cinematography by Svetlana Cvetko and Kalyanee Mam is excellent. The use of graphics helps make points and explain issues. Sound design is effective. Because of the controversial nature of the interviews, it seems appropriate that the questions being asked by the interviewer are often heard off-camera. No one can claim that their answers to the questions were taken out of context.

Note: At various times in U.S. history, political views have become highly polarized. The nonfiction "advocacy" context of political-style documentaries is stretched, making much of what is produced pure propaganda. Documentaries of lasting meaning should strive to examine and explore reality based on facts, not distortions, character assassination, and partisan political agendas.

Documentaries may crossover into more than one category. Academy Award-winning documentary, *The Fog of War* is a historical, educational, social, and political documentary with a distinct journalistic style. In this documentary, director Errol Morris, with the help of editors Karen Schmeer, Doug Abel, and Chyld King, takes an intimate conversation with Robert S McNamara and brings it to life using archival footage, effects, and music that complements McNamara's story. In an introduction to the eleven lessons discussed in the documentary, McNamara states that he is "at an age where I can look back and derive some conclusions about my actions. My rule has been to try to learn, understand what happened, develop the lessons, and pass them on...." The documentary is structured so that McNamara can convey insight derived from his experience in life.

The Fog Of War - Eleven Lessons From The Life Of Robert S. McNamara is more than lessons about the cruelty of war. McNamara and director Errol Morris explore issues surrounding war, including the mindset, ethics, politics, and mistakes made in US policy decisions during the life of Robert S. McNamara. The documentary begins with a montage of war scenes and film credits, set to original music by Philip Glass. Soon Robert S. McNamara, former Secretary of Defense under President Kennedy and President Johnson is seen sitting in what appears to be a sound recording booth talking to Errol Morris, who is heard off camera while conducting the conversation. What follows is a unique, insightful story built around the life experience of McNamara, born in San Francisco, California, at the end of the First World War. The documentary is based on McNamara's book of the same name.

McNamara includes information about his career, personal history, and controversial background. As the documentary progresses, McNamara reflects on past events that influenced him. This provides a sense of his identity and what he has experienced to bring him to these conclusions. Morris uses his conversation with McNamara to narrate the documentary. Talking to Morris, McNamara looks directly at the camera. Occasionally, we hear an exchange or question between Morris and McNamara.

Unlike other films by Errol Morris, this film stays in the nonfiction documentary category with no reenactments. Using McNamara's interview with archival footage is dramatic and informative. In some ways, this is similar to the style Ken

Burns uses in his documentaries. Morris may use music more dramatically and editorially than Burns, bringing out some of the tension inherent in the archival footage and McNamara's voice-over. In addition to McNamara, dialog from others is heard in the archival footage. For example, audio conversations between John F. Kennedy and his advisers are used during the Cuban Missile Crisis sequences. Later, during the Vietnam War, Lyndon Johnson is heard in previously taped recordings. *The Fog Of War,* as a documentary, is significant from a historical, political, cultural, and educational perspective. This documentary supports the notion that "those who do not learn from the past are doomed to repeat the same mistakes repeatedly."

Fired-up - Public Housing is My Home is an Emmy award-winning documentary that looks at possible solutions to problems concerning urban public housing in major cities, focusing on Chicago. Supported by the Metropolitan Planning Council (MPC), a not-for-profit foundation, tenants in public housing undertake a two-year learning process to see if a concept known as "tenant management" will help to change living conditions in high-rise public housing developments like Cabrini Green. To help with training and education, Bertha Gilkey, a successful leader of tenant management in Saint Louis, is brought in to help the tenants learn how to manage the buildings.

An independent documentary filmmaker, James R. Martin, the author of this book, is given a grant by the Metropolitan Planning Council (MPC) to document the process. Mary Decker, CEO of MPC, provides the filmmaker with absolute creative control of making the documentary. As the project proceeds, interviews with all concerned, seminars, training, successful tenant management in Saint Louis, and general progress are documented. The documentary is edited chronologically as training and events proceed during the project. There is a mixture of interviews, events, seminars, historic photographs, and conflicting opinions voiced by board members managing Chicago's public housing. The final sixty-minute documentary was broadcast nationally in the United States on Public Television. Unfortunately, Tenant Management did not catch on in Chicago. High-rise public housing buildings, including those at Cabrini Green, are ultimately torn down entirely by 2010. This project is an example of how a private source can finance an independent documentary project if they give the filmmakers creative control of telling the story.

Educational

Most documentaries are "educational" in some respect. This includes subjects that may be of educational interest to the general public or for use in education at all levels. Nonfiction explorations that deal with educational issues also fit into this area. An educational documentary must have educational priorities and information conveyed for this purpose. Educational documentaries need to be propaganda-free and seek to shed light on the subjects discussed factually. Academic inquiry on a given topic can strive to be objectively neutral.

Public Television (PBS) in the U.S. has consistently aired educational documentaries in all categories. The Chinese Exclusion Act, a part of the American Experience series on PBS, has relevance in many areas, including history, ethnic studies, politics, government, and other humanities disciplines

The Chinese Exclusion Act, a Steeplechase Documentary, 2018, directed by Ric Burns and Li-Shin Yu, looks at the history of Chinese immigrants to the United States and their sixty-year exclusion from becoming citizens even when they were born in the U.S. The Exclusion Act, made into U.S. law in 1882, came after forty years of discrimination and harassment of Chinese coming to California for the Gold Rush and to work on building the Trans-Continental Railroad leg from California to Utah. In the case of the railroad, Chinese workers were encouraged to migrate from China to California. The Chinese were treated far worse than European immigrants, like the Irish and Italians, who were also mistreated. However, European Immigrants never had an "Exclusion Act" to deal with and complete prohibition from any path to citizenship or guarantee of fundamental human rights. The Chinese Exclusion Act was not repealed until 1943, when China and the US became allies against the Japanese in World War II. The current immigration laws in the US were enacted in the 1960s.

The Chinese Exclusion Act 2018 documentary, edited by Li-Shin Yu, mostly conforms to the same editing style seen in Ken Burns' (Ric's Brother) films. Archival photographs and other documentation combined with expert interviews, historians, voice-over narration, music, and effects tell the story. There is an interesting use of audio effects in the documentary. Subtle presence tracks supporting the photographs are often heard under the voice-over narration. This adds depth and reality to the pictures used and the story.

The pace is excellent, and the two-hour documentary opens up an aspect of U.S. history that only a few people know. Information about The Chinese Exclusion Act may be difficult to find in American History Books. The documentary does not directly reference current anti-immigrant rhetoric; however, the similarity is apparent. By exploring this issue, the documentary can help all Americans see how history repeats itself. The documentary also reveals the deep-rooted tribalism that emboldens racist and ethnic hostility. *The Chinese Exclusion Act* is an educational documentary about American History, Chinese American History, and a clear look at racial attitudes in the U.S. It also examines how politics and politicians can manipulate people to turn against others. This story is an "eye-opener" about the early Chinese American experience and its connection to the country's history.

Mental Health

Documentaries that look at how people live with stress, disease, afflictions, handicaps, mental illness, psychological problems, and the institutions mandated to care for them. Frederick Wiseman's 1967 documentary, Titicut Follies, is about the patients of Bridgewater State Hospital, an institution for the mentally disturbed. Titicut Follies shows the daily life of the inmates of the State Hospital who are left in empty cells with no sanitation or personal hygiene. Patients are force-fed, stripped naked in public, and bullied by the staff. Wiseman and John Marshal, his cameraman, are given free rein to film everything they find at the Bridgewater State Hospital. The finished documentary was banned from being seen in Massachusetts and other places for some time because of the graphic depiction of the maltreatment of the inmates. Wiseman uses a "Direct Cinema" approach to making the documentary. There are no formal interviews. The camera is the observing eye, "the fly on the wall."

Health and Medical Issues

Disease, drugs, nutrition, health, diet, and related areas. These documentaries explore medical and health issues facing civilization.

Sicko, , made in 2007 and directed by Michael Moore, is a theatrical documentary that compares healthcare in the United States, France, Great Britain, and Canada. Moore humorously compares services and costs in each country by speaking with people and medical professionals in each place. Moore acts as host and is seen on camera as he is in all his other documentaries. The documentary's point of view is that healthcare availability and costs in the United States are far below the standards in other countries. This point of view is substantiated in the film. It is a well-made advocacy documentary for universal health care in the United States. While the comparisons tend to be one-sided, it is clear that healthcare services in other countries are not affordable or available in the United States.

Forks Over Knives 2011 is written and directed by Lee Folkerson, who looks at the effect of processed and animal-based foods on his health for personal reasons. The research of Dr. T. Colin Campbell, a nutritional biochemist from Cornell University, and Dr. Caldwell Esselstyn, a former surgeon at the well know Cleveland Clinic, are highlighted. According to the filmmaker, Esselystyn and Campbell's separate, independent studies into degenerative diseases prove a connection between eating processed and animal-based foods and diseases like type 2 diabetes, heart disease, cancer, and other problems.

The opening scene of *Forks Over Knives* starts with the following quote, "the average American now carries twenty-three extra pounds." "Heart disease and stroke will claim the lives of four-hundred-sixty-thousand American Women," and "We're talking about diabetes and hypertension, bone disease and osteoporosis" Facts are presented about the food Americans eat and health problems in the United States and other countries.

Food and the drugs Americans take may be highly harmful to the health of adults and children in the long run. According to the film, the US spends five times more on health care than the defense budget. Why are there so many health problems? Bill Maher says, "...There's no money in healthy people or dead people. The people in the middle live with one or more chronic conditions." Additional people, including Michele Obama, talk about "Obesity" and other conditions as seen in a montage of film clips. The facts are well documented, and the problems are well stated to justify the investigation conducted by the documentary. One of the marks of a good documentary story is not to have a string of talking head interviews. In Forks Over Knives, there is a continuing montage of action and "B" roll that parallels what is claimed with graphic evidence making for a convincing argument.

Forks Over Knives takes an unexpected turn when it goes to China and finds a study done there, initiated by Chinese Premier Zhou En-lai, who suffered from bladder cancer. Six hundred and fifty thousand researchers cataloged the mortality patterns caused by several types of cancer between 1973 and 1975. The study covered every county in China and over eight-hundred-fifty-million people. Based on the analysis, Dr. Campbell found crucial correlations between what people in China ate and the types of cancer and other diseases they contracted. An in-depth food and nutrition study ensued, looking at the diet and lifestyles of people over many years. The results were conclusive. In 1990 after ten years of intensive work, Dr. Campbell and his team published the China Study. It identified no less than ninety-four thousand correlations between diet and disease.

Sound and Fury, directed by Josh Aronson, is the story of Heather Artinian, a young deaf girl caught up between the opportunity to hear after a surgical implant operation and the opposition to it by her extended family and the deaf community who accept deafness as a way of life. Heather, her deaf parents, hearing siblings, and non-hearing and hearing grandparents are caught up in the issues and politics of giving Heather the ability to hear through a surgical implant known as a cochlear implant. (CI), a surgically implanted electronic device that provides a sense of sound to a person who is profoundly deaf or severely hard of hearing.

As a documentary, *Sound and Fury* may fall under a medical category. However, it is also educational, cultural, social, and in certain aspects, anthropological. It brings the "deaf community" into focus as one in which people do not consider themselves handicapped. They are a subgroup in the culture. Sound and Fury is a moving, insightful documentary that is well-edited and filmed. The documentary allows all the arguments, pros, and cons of the cochlear implanting of Heather. Also, what it means to her parents and others concerned. Peter's hearing brother and his hearing wife give birth to twins, one of whom is deaf. Chris and Mari go through the process of learning about cochlear implants and decide to proceed with the operation. Heather's mother, who is now apparently leaning against the implant, argues with Mari to the extent that you wonder why she is against this operation. Marianne, Heather's Grandmother, is for Heather getting the implant and pushes her son Peter to do this for Heather. The filmmakers have put together a story that explores the issues and conflicts without distorting the actuality the subjects face.

PUBLIC SERVICE SECTOR

Documentaries that focus on civil service occupations like firefighters, police, canine corps, and other civil service work.

Why do people choose these careers? Also, events that local government agencies sponsor.

FAMILY

Relationships, dysfunctional and functional, family histories, oral histories, and generational conflicts. Oral histories may be combined with recorded interviews and photographs to make a documentary about a family or community. These stories usually include psychologists, social workers, and other experts. The documentary Sound and Fury fits into the Family category in many respects.

SPORTS

Documentaries about the world of sports competition and training. What they mean, why people participate or do not, and stories about sports teams from little league and adult amateur to professional.

Undefeated, a 2011 Oscar winner for Best Feature Documentary, is a story about what happens when one man's passion ignites a chain of events that changes everything it touches. This documentary looks at life, relationships, character, stereotypes, high school sports, and the will to win as more than a football game victory. Directors Dan Lindsay and TJ Martin read an article about a young high school football player from Memphis who is being mentored academically by his coaches at the coach's homes because tutors would not go into his neighborhood at night. They thought this might make an interesting documentary. However, as they explored the idea, they discovered a bigger story. Manassas High School, founded in 1899, had never had a winning season playing football. They had not won a game in fourteen years! Other high schools in Tennessee have been known to pay them to come to their schools to give their teams a practice dummy. Bill Courtney volunteered as a coach in 2004 and began shaping students into a team. After six years of working, recruiting players, and infusing them with his philosophy and brand of inspirational guidance, he has a team that's capable of having a winning season. But there are still issues with players whose personal lives and misfortunes must be overcome.

Undefeated is a narrative-style documentary. The directors had a vision for the story they wanted to tell. The environment, school, meetings, home life, and games coverage are excellent, with action that provides intimacy and information. The editing keeps the pace of the one-hundred-twelve-minute documentary moving. The storytelling builds on the natural conflict and drama of the subjects and their quest for a championship. Music and effects add to the story. In most instances, the filmmakers made themselves almost invisible to the subjects who interacted as if there was no camera.

Current or Topical Issues

Who cares about high gasoline prices, and why do they rise and fall at the drop of any crisis? Why did it take so long for modern electric cars to become available? What is the impact of using "fracking" for natural gas drilling? Topics may include alternative energy sources, urban life, nightlife in the city, local museums, places of interest, apartment living, and first-person stories involving current cultural issues. *Who Killed The Electric Car* is a documentary examining how General Motors and other auto companies, forced to build an electric car by California laws in the 1980s, took all the vehicles off the market as soon as the law expired and destroyed them.

Gasland, a 2010 Academy award nominated documentary, takes the form of a personal journey by the filmmaker to discover what "fracking" technology is all about and what it is doing to the environment. This documentary is an advocacy documentary about a current issue. This documentary is interesting because it's a personal story of discovery for Josh Fox, the film's director. He narrates much of the film, beginning with his first encounter with the natural gas industry. At that time, he receives an offer from a natural gas drilling company to lease his land in Pennsylvania for drilling. Based on his love for the environment where he grew up, he begins to investigate what drilling on his land might mean despite the one-hundred-thousand dollar offer he has received.

The rest of the film is based on his travels to drilling sites in twenty-four states nationwide. What he discovers is devastating, including flammable tap water! Along with Josh, you get to meet individuals and families, all with stories concerning their well water before and after the hydraulic fracturing process used to free the natural gas from the shale 8000 feet below the surface is used. "Fracking," as the process is called, blasts a mixture of more than five-hundred and ninety-six chemicals and water to fracture the rock, releasing the gas. The documentary doesn't just voice complaints; it shows the problem and the results time after time. If you've never seen water pouring from the tap that can be lit with a match, you will see it in *Gasland*.

Gasland has a point of view that is obvious. However, it does endeavor to present the industry claims that there has been no impact from the hydraulic fracture process. No one in the industry wants to discuss the process of using many carcinogenic chemicals and enormous amounts of water. Much of the chemicals and water stay in the ground, polluting nearby residents' water tables and wells. Residents offer glasses of the toxic well water to company officials when they visit. These officials claim the water is safe to drink. The officials declined the offer.

The camera work is fundamental, handheld, and from the filmmaker's POV, but this "guerilla" style of documentary filmmaking gives the story the intimacy Cinéma vérité offers. There is a second camera when we see Josh Fox shooting. Most of the documentary feels spontaneous. One dubious scene toward the end with a slide projected on a wall seems more like an homage to An Inconvenient Truth than anything else. Editing is well-paced. The sound design, including banjo playing by Josh Fox, is appropriate.

In a documentary production where you have a great deal of coverage, including interviews and archival material gathered spontaneously, it's essential to find a way to structure the story to include a beginning, middle, and end. Find the issues and conflicts in the story. *Gasland* achieves this by developing parallel themes and creating some anticipation regarding the outcomes and even the validity of some of the claims made by the subjects interviewed, including the government and one company official. Josh's quest is paralleled by the experience of the people he meets. For the first twenty-three minutes of the documentary, you wonder if there is flammable tap water. These factors keep up interest and bring you into the story.

Reminiscent of films by Michael Moore, *Gasland* fits into the same genre as other personal advocacy documentaries where the filmmaker involves him or herself in the story. In many respects, the technique feels like a nonfiction book, making its point of view clear up-front. There are also many first-person accounts and graphic examples of the results of natural gas drilling using hydraulic fracturin.g

GENDER ISSUES
Specifically, all gender rights, and lifestyles.

The Invisible War, Academy Award Nominee in 2013, reveals a tragic story. The Invisible War is an investigative documentary on the high rate of rape, sexual assault, and abuse of women in the US military. The documentary uses interviews with military women, experts, and others combined with archival footage of women in the military testifying at congressional hearings to explore the issue. The stories of each woman run in parallel as their husbands and families are introduced. The women all suffer greatly from post-traumatic stress syndrome. Many have medical problems resulting from savage attacks. According to the documentary, "over twenty percent of female veterans have been sexually assaulted while serving" (in the military).

The documentary presents interviews with the victims of these crimes. Journalists like Amy Herdy, author of "Betrayal in the Ranks," is seen giving facts and information about this tragedy in the military. Ms. Herdy talks about the number of actual assaults being much higher because women don't report them for fear of reprisals. She estimates that half a million women have been sexually assaulted in the military. But the sexual assaults are not just limited to women. Men have suffered from these assaults as well. Invisible War makes a strong case that there are sexual predators who get away with it while in the military and, when discharged, continue doing it. They stalk their victims, often being individuals whom no one would suspect. The Invisible War is an extremely well-made documentary investigating a significant problem in the United States military. This type of documentary can and does often promote change. For example, after watching The Invisible War, Leon Panetta, then the Secretary of Defense, decided to prosecute offenders away from unit commanders.

Women and Spirituality - - The Goddess Trilogy is a three-part series of documentaries exploring women's role throughout prehistory, early, and more recent history. Part I looks at prehistory and evidence, beginning with stone age culture, where carved Goddess sculptures and cave paintings are found in France. The Mother Earth creation story, along with the nurturing role of women in peaceful hunter-gather groups, is established. Part 2 covers the years between 10,000 to 1500 BCE. Using graphic art from this period and interviews with historians, the documentary demonstrates the impact of the "Witch Craze" on the status of women ever since those days. There was no room in Christianity at that period for powerful women. All types of things were blamed on women, including plagues and the failure of crops. During this time, a strong case is made for the notion that female sexuality is evil. Violence and sex are linked. Female spirituality is branded as witchcraft and connected with the devil. Part 3 deals with Goddess worship though out the ages.

Women and Spirituality, sponsored by the National Film Board of Canada, is a well-made documentary series presenting its straightforward viewpoint. It advocates female spirituality. It offers historical information that leaves little doubt that Goddess Worship and religion centered around female divinity have been suppressed over the ages. This educational documentary sheds light on the status of women in mainly western society today as a result of history. It offers a view of women that needs to be understood today.

Like many strong advocacy documentary efforts, there is a tendency to present facts with little substantiation beyond generalizations. Assumptions based on these ideas become vague in places. Speculation about prehistoric cultures and their religious practices appears to be based on beautifully carved statuettes of women that embody the traditional attitude of prehistoric people toward women. This interpretation is speculative about what may have been. To the credit of the documentary, evidence indicates that prehistoric people respected and worshiped female spirituality.

Women and Spirituality, The Goddess Trilogy, offers a substantial body of information that must be addressed. It makes a convincing case for female spirituality and the fundamental role of women in religion, life, and possibly saving Mother Earth, our home, from destruction.

Religion

The secular and non-secular documentary exploration of religious and spiritual topics. The role religion plays in life and the history of religion and religious culture.

Devils Playground, directed by Lucy Walker, explores a coming-of-age tradition in the Amish Religion. Amish sixteen-year-old young adults practice "Rumspringa" (running around) in the "English" world, aka "Devil's Playground." This is done before deciding whether to be baptized into the Amish Religion. Devil's Playground is a documentary structured and edited in a way that pulls the viewer into the actuality of the subject's experience. The story is told narratively in three acts.

There does not appear to be any apparent exaggeration or staging of events. Editing allows the action and interviews with the subjects to be presented as a story. This type of nonfiction presentation relies on Direct Cinema style shooting and additional interviews. The story comes together in the editing room. With certain reservations, the documentary has anthropological overtones as "salvage" anthropology or ethnography. *Devil's Playground* gives honest insight into the Amish community and "Rumspringa" as the teenagers experience it. It is important to note that ninety percent of the young adults decide to become part of the Amish religion after this experience. One contributing factor to this high rate may be that their Amish families are supportive, and being baptized into the faith brings security and shelter from the outside world.

Personal Journeys

This type of documentary takes on an autobiographical nature. They are often a story about some life-changing event in the director's world. This turning point may be religious, philosophical, or educational. One example is *I AM*, directed by Tom Shadyac, whose films include Bruce The Almighty, Ace Ventura: Pet Detective, and The Nutty Professor. Making a documentary is a significant departure for him. At this point in his career, Shadyac has it all: luxurious homes, corporate jets, and the rich and famous lifestyle, until one day, he is in an accident riding his bicycle. The concussion he receives in the accident puts him in the hospital for an extended stay. Even after being released from the hospital, he suffers from Post-Concussion Syndrome, the same type of malady pro football players experience. When he finally recovers, he decides to find the answer to two key questions. "What is wrong with our world?" And "what can we do about it?" With a small documentary film crew of four, Shadyac goes on a quest to find the answer to these questions by interviewing some notable thinkers, including authors, poets, teachers, religious leaders, and scientists (Lynn McTaggart, Desmond Tutu, Thom Harman, Coleman Barks, David Zuzuki and others).

> "We started asking what's wrong with the world and ended up discovering what's right with it." -- Tom Shadyac.

Shadyac sets up this hybrid documentary with what may be reenacted scenes of him in the hospital, leaving the hospital, and recovering. Before long there are shots of his past opulent Hollywood life style with one or two large, nouveau riche decorated homes. This opening seems a little long but does make the point of how rich Shadyac is and how he seems to have been, like many Americans, obsessed with material wealth. But the central theme of this story is not material wealth. It also appears that Shadyac "lived the life" because he thought it was what you were supposed to do.

I AM covers contemporary issues about how we live. The film brings to light the problems and offers possible solutions. It is fast-paced and incorporates archival footage and graphics to tell the story. Director Tom Shadyac chose to treat the story as a personal quest. At times he looks pretty self-conscious in this role. *I AM* is a documentary that makes many worthwhile observations about how people live. It thoughtfully examines values and what might be done to reverse some of the more dangerous trends in the current version of civilization. *I AM* is paced well and makes its point of view known early in the story. The story explores how people have evolved a perception of themselves and the world around them. One central theme is that Homo sapiens have survived, not necessarily by "survival of the fittest," but by cooperation with others. Only one aspect of Darwin's Theory of Evolution is studied. His theories about cooperation as part of human survival and evolution have been ignored. What emerges is the idea that humans have separated themselves from nature so completely that it could be self-destructive. Science evolves in its theories, but the documentary claims that there may be over-reliance on science in our culture.

> In his novel "Island," Aldus Huxley wrote: "Dualism... Without it, there can hardly be good literature. With it, there most certainly can be no good life. "I" affirms a separate and abiding me-substance; "am" denies the fact that all existence is relationship and change. "I am." Two tiny words, but what an enormity of untruth! The religiously minded dualist calls homemade spirits from the vastly deep; the nondualist calls the vastly deep into his spirit or, to be more accurate, he finds that the vastly deep is already there.[1]"

Interestingly, a famous filmmaker made a documentary that talks about humans cooperating. That's what filmmakers do making films. They collaborate to create something more significant than the sum of its parts, which wasn't there before.

PORTRAITS

Profiles or portraits about the lives of individuals, families, or groups. Lives that are successful, not so successful. Lives of those who have lived a long time and those who have not. How people from all walks of life got to where they are now. How and why they do their jobs and live their lives. Like a portrait painting, documentary portraits can have many subtle dimensions. At first, you might not think *BUCK*, a documentary about a "horse whisperer," would have universal appeal. But once you start to watch this documentary, you realize it has appeal on many

---

[1] In Buddhist teaching there is "no self." Therefore no "I" or "am."

levels. Buck Brannaman is a horse whisperer, a real one. He and his methods are unique and built on his life experience. He's a sincere, unpretentious cowboy with a philosophy from which everyone can learn. BUCK tells a story that transcends the point of view perspective of many documentary films that deal with humanistic, social, or advocacy issues.

Directed by Cindy Meehl, BUCK incorporates footage of Buck Brannaman working with horses at clinics nationwide. He teaches the attendees how to deal with horses in an empathetic fashion. In one scene, he explains what it might feel like to a horse when someone jumps on its back. He explains that's the way a lion would attack a horse. It jumps on the horse's back, bites, and uses its claws to open up the horse's neck. So instinctively, the horse has some built-in apprehension on that score. The horse needs to overcome instinctive fear to be able to trust anyone. Punishing the horse because it doesn't do what it is told makes it more fearful.

The story combines footage of Buck Brannaman in action at clinics, interviews, and events—archival photographs and videos of Buck over the years. The film is edited in a way that answers questions before you think of them and moves the narrative along at a comfortable pace. The cinematography is intimate, and the camera there when the action happens. Sound design and music work well throughout the film.

Media

Documentaries that look at the role of Media in today's world. Films like Orwell Rolls in His Grave. "Who controls the past, controls the future - who controls the present controls the past." -- Orwell, 1984. Using quotes from George Orwell's novel

1984, the documentary film Orwell Rolls In His Grave, written, directed, and edited by Robert Kane Pappas, explores media's role in today's world. It is a prophetic documentary conveying a message that seems even more urgent today than when the film was made in 2004. Orwell Rolls In His Grave asks controversial questions about the political and corporate control of the public's need to know. Pappas, aided by many knowledgeable people, deconstructs events in recent history bringing to light what they believe is the Orwellian world of modern life.

The film poses many questions. Are we living in what we might call a "mediocracy?" Has the media become the authority for what news and information reach the public? Is "news" about the events and people covered, or is it about marketing for viewership? These and many other topics are looked at in depth. Orwell Rolls In His Grave includes clips of Michael Moore speaking, interviews with Representative Bernie Sanders of Vermont, Charles Lewis, director of the Center for Public Integrity, Greg Palast, author of The Best Democracy Money Can Buy, Vincent Bugliosi, former Los Angeles: prosecutor and legal scholar, and many others. Interviews in Orwell Rolls In His Grave are combined with graphics, narration, news clips, statistics, quotes, archival film, and photographs to create a narrative that appears to have come true in life, right here in the United States and perhaps the world. Aside from ominous, dramatic music underscoring quotes from Orwell and other scenes, the film does not try to manipulate the audience. Given the evidence presented, it presents facts, asks questions, and supports a point of view that is difficult to dispute.

One of the topics explored in Orwell Rolls In His Grave is how the media rolled over covering the 2000 U.S. national election during the dispute over whether Al Gore or G.W. Bush won in Florida. In another instance, the film asks why the media has not looked into issues about the massive rise in wealth for a small number of Americans while most citizens have seen a decrease in earnings. Who owns the media comes to mind?

"If you repeat a lie often enough people will believe it."
-- Joesph Goebbels

Orwell Rolls In His Grave is a social, historical, and advocacy documentary statement. It asks questions and explores issues using an objective reality format that presents actuality in a way that provokes thought about the world we live in today. This documentary removes the foggy eyeglasses issued by indifference and spin to show a world that would make *Orwell Roll In His Grave*.

Entertainment

Documentaries about performances of music, concerts, and other entertainment events. What do people do for entertainment, unusual or new activities? Documentaries that explore forms of entertainment that evolve out of cultural trends. Documentaries about the Entertainment Industry may cross over into other categories. One such documentary is *20 Feet From Stardom* which explores the experience of women in the recording industry, specifically background singers, who are the vocalists behind lead singers.

In the opening segment of *20 Feet From Stardom*, Bruce Springsteen says, "it's a pretty long walk from background singer to lead... a walk to the front is complicated." *20 Feet From Stardom* is a documentary film celebrating special people who help make beautiful music. Winner of an Oscar for Best Feature

Documentary at the 2014 Academy Awards, 20 Feet From Stardom, directed by Morgan Neville, introduces the women (and one man) whose voices will be recognized immediately, even if you don't know their names. But this is more than an introduction and some interviews reminiscing about the good old days. *20 Feet From Stardom* presents performance after performance, where background vocalists create the depth and feel of each song. Along with hearing the vocalists, their art's history, struggles, and evolution unfolds. *20 Feet From Stardom* cinematography, by Nicola Marsh and Graham Willoughby, is excellent. Editing new and archival footage by Douglas Blush, Kevin Klauber, and Jason Zeldes is also excellent. The ninety-minute documentary is structured around interviews, performances past and present, and clips of the singers as they are today.

Introduced in *20 Feet From Stardom* is the woman who has been the female vocalist on every Rolling Stones album since 1989. Parallel stories unfold of her and many other great talents from early to recent days. Meet Darlene Love, The Blossoms, Merry Clayton, Judith Hill, Claudia Lennear, Lisa Fisher, Tata Vega, The Waters, and many others. Learn about their relationships with the lead singers they work with, including David Bowie and the Talking Heads, Sting, Bruce Springsteen, Ray Charles, Stevie Wonder, Joe Cocker, Luther Vandross, Mick Jagger, Bette Midler, and others. Like all good documentaries, a compelling story is told that is entertaining and educational

Science

NOVA is an American series of documentaries that explores science-related subjects. WGBH Boston has produced it for the U.S. Public Broadcasting System (PBS) since 1974. Not all of the documentaries are made in the United States. Many programs are picked up by WGBH and adapted for the American audience. One source is the BBC. More recent documentaries have been produced with National Geographic and other cable channels. NOVA documentaries look at a wide variety of subjects.

The basic format combines action, narration, interviews, graphics, simulation or recreation of events, photographs, archival materials, and music. A dramatic structure is often applied to the scientific process creating plot conflict around exploration, discovery, and conclusions. Once a subject is chosen, a concept, treatment, and script are written based on available material and events that may still be happening. A script might also be written based entirely on available footage, archival material, and other sources. The approach used in the NOVA documentary programs is also widely used for non-scientific subjects like history, nature, and educational documentaries.

NASA

For All Mankind is an independently produced, theatrically released documentary. *For All Mankind*, directed by Al Reinert, is a compilation documentary that uses footage shot entirely by The National Aeronautics & Space Administration (NASA) over the years of the mission to reach the moon. Edited by Susan Karda, the documentary captures a trip to the moon and the spirit of the astronauts who journeyed. *For All Mankind* is an exciting documentary that takes you back in time as you travel to the moon with the astronauts who were there. The entire film uses the first-person narration of many astronauts speaking at the time or reflecting on their experience afterward. In addition, footage of the Houston Command Center and the dialog between the astronauts and mission control is used. Original Music by Brian

Eno, plus recordings the astronauts took with them, complete the musical score.

For All Mankind is historical, using archival footage shot at the time to build a story that takes the viewer on a trip to the moon. First, experience the dramatic lift off, next the leaving of Earth orbit at six thousand feet per second, traveling to, and ultimately orbiting the moon. Once in moon orbit, go with the astronauts in the moon lander as it settles gently on the moon's surface. On the moon, witness that famous "small step for man, a giant step for mankind" with Neil Armstrong and his walk on the moon.

For All Mankind does a great job recreating the traveling to the moon experience. This includes the feeling the astronauts experience leaving the planet, seeing it grow smaller as they move farther away from its blue oceans. There are no longer countries and continents, just one Mother Earth. It also shows life in the command module as the astronauts deal with weightlessness in this tiny spaceship. For All Mankind is a fantastic documentary that humanizes space travel and exhibits the uniqueness of humankind and the planet Earth.

TRAINING

Documentary format training films and videos for sports and other areas, including vocational training, crafts, military training videos, corporate training films, videos, and multimedia presentations. Using a documentary format for a training presentation can add a new dimension to the learning curve.

First Position is a documentary showing how intense training can be for children in one profession. *First Position* is about the rigors faced by children and young adults, both male and female, as they train to become ballet dancers. The story explores the lives of six or seven main characters, from a seven-year-old boy to a seventeen-year-old girl who is about to graduate from high school. They all train and ultimately compete in various competitions. The documentary also explores parent and trainer involvement, the environment, and the stress placed on all involved.

"First Position" is the basic stance for a Ballerina or Ballet Dancer. The subjects of First Position, the documentary, are young people who are beginning their careers as dancers in a dance form that is demanding physically and mentally in every way. Many dancers begin training at four or five years of age and never stop until their careers as dancers end, often by the time they are thirty-five. First Position, directed by Bess Kargman, whom herself trained in ballet, shows great sensitivity to a multitude of issues involved in the dedication and discipline it takes to become a ballet dancer. The film explores the young dancers' worlds, including their interaction with parents and teachers. The documentary examines the process of training and competing in The Youth American Gran Prix International Competition, where young dancers can win scholarships and offers to join dance companies worldwide. Five thousand dancers compete in preliminary competitions, but only about two hundred will get to go to New York. Each person's story is engaging and unique. Together they contribute to an in-depth story. As the documentary progresses, the viewer gets to know each of the characters involved. When the competitions occur, it feels like all of them should win.

Several cinematic elements make First Position a successful documentary and nonfiction story. First Position's natural dramatic structure evokes emotion and drama from the beginning. The stories of the dancers are filled with conflict and obstacles they have endured and must overcome each day. In essentially three acts, Kargman tells a story in which young dancers struggle for perfection against long odds within the environment where they live and work. Ultimately, they face performing in a competition that could change their lives. A happy ending for everyone in this tale is not a given. As an observer in this story, you feel the emotions and struggles of these young performers and the people who support them. Ultimately you are drawn from casual observer to emotional participant in the ongoing documentary actuality.

There is fluid and moving cinematography by Director of Photography and Cinematographer Nick Higgins. The film appears to have been shot in a high-definition digital format. It looks good on a theater's big screen. Excellent coverage of rehearsals, training, backstage activity, performance, and audience reaction exists. Covering dancers' performances on a stage showing their movements in a long shot and with close-ups for detail is challenging. *First Position* gives the audience perspective of the performance, on-stage intimacy occasionally, and the dancers behind the scenes point of view to open up the experience.

Editor Kate Amend does a fantastic job keeping the pace and flow of the documentary moving based on action and not just interviews and "B" roll. A story about dance needs action, not just people talking about dance. To the credit of Kargman and Higgins, action coverage is available to tell the story. Interviews, both first-person and observational dialog, narrates the action. The score composed by Chris Hajian supports the subject of the film and adds another dimension to the story. The audio mix of First Position includes the actual ambient sounds of the action, with effects, music, and interviews that give a feeling of actuality and being there.

OBSERVER

The Chronicling and observing of events, subjects, and various happenings of interest. This point of view allows for a first-person interpretation of reality. Direct Cinema and Cinéma vérité formats bring the viewer into the story as an observer.

Manufactured Landscapes, directed by Jennifer Baichwal, and photographed by Edward Burtynsky, begins with an eight-minute track of a seemingly endless manufacturing floor with row after row of assembly tables staffed by Chinese workers in yellow shirts. This takes up about ten percent of this ninety-minute documentary. There's a rule of thumb in filmmaking: even if you're trying to depict boredom, you can't bore your audience. In this case, a "manufacturing landscape" is shown. After sixty seconds of this opening tracking shot, everyone should "get it!" The following seven minutes-thirty seconds are repetitive. As mentioned previously, documentary filmmaker Ken Burns has said, "at times it's good to hold the shot, [that] meaning accrues in duration." The "meaning" of this shot accrues in about ten seconds!

The redeeming value of the documentary is that both the cinematography and Burtynsky's photography are excellent. The documentary explores industrial landscapes in China and, in one sequence, a beach in Bangladesh, where they salvage ships for scrap. The problem with *Manufactured Landscapes* is the difference between observing a still photograph hanging on a wall and watching a film. You can stand as long as you want in front of a photograph, take it in, and move on when ready. But with a film, the audience is captive, so you can't have everyone sit there with the same static shot, even to make a point, because once the audience reads the scene, they will lose interest if nothing new happens. The reverse is also true. The viewer must have enough time to read the shot. There is a rhythm and pattern to editing. In addition, film is a medium that requires action and reaction. The time for a cut is when the action ends. The fact that the camera is in motion, recording a static situation, does not create a movement that's not there in the scene.

Overall, the pace of this film feels like visiting a museum and looking at the work on the walls. After a while, there can be sensory overload and a need to take a break. There are scenes of people walking around a museum gallery looking at Burtynsky's photographs. Sometimes, the filmmakers are heard discussing the shot, setting up shots, and just being in the film. It all seems a bit self-indulgent with no apparent purpose except in one sequence where Chinese officials are seen trying to stop Burtynsky from taking photographs of the coal mining process in China. The imagery in *Manufactured Landscapes* is solid and vivid. For example, the shots and scenes showing the massive equipment and resources used to construct the Three Gorges Dam in China are compositions that convey the textures and patterns of this mammoth and controversial undertaking.

The film shows several scenes in black and white for no apparent reason. Black and white, essentially shades of gray, are technically an abstraction since most humans perceive the world in color. Shifting between abstraction and reality should have a clear purpose in the story. In *Manufactured Landscapes*, it seems like a device with no particular significance beyond a transition to introduce color into the scene. The black and white shots possibly had faulty colors that could not be corrected.

Even with the lack of cinematic storytelling technique, *Manufactured Landscapes* is worth watching. This montage allows one to experience these industrial landscapes and their environmental impact. Also, to observe the people who live in those surroundings. Burtynsky states that he is not attempting to judge what is shown as good or bad. He presents it so the viewer can make up their mind.

JOURNALISTIC

This area includes topical news-based stories in the tradition of Edward R. Murrow, Fred Friendly, 60 Minutes, Front Line, and cable channels like MSNBC, CNN, and VICE. Harvest of Shame is a classic television documentary produced by David Lowe, CBS, narrated by Edward R. Murrow, about migrant farm workers. It was broadcast nationally on Thanksgiving Day in 1960. *Harvest of Shame* was prevented from being distributed beyond the initial television broadcast because of its candid description of problems regarding migrant farm workers in the United States. Later investigative documentaries by CBS included those about Senator Joseph McCarthy and the McCarthy hearings. These early television documentaries employed an on-camera interviewer and narrator

CORPORATE

Internal corporate documentaries about manufacturing, testing, training, or product lines. At one time, corporations sponsored documentaries about different subjects, distributed them to schools, and often played them in theaters as short subjects. Short documentaries or short fictional films are no longer screened in theaters. Many large corporations have in-house production departments that produce documentaries for internal use

INFORMATIONAL

Public Service Announcement (PSA) documentaries usually provide some information about a not-for-profit, charity, or government agency to inform the general public on issues or concerns.

PUBLIC RELATIONS

Documentaries acquainting the public with an individual, firm, institution, or corporation, including documentary-style "infomercials and soft commercial videos.

DOCUDRAMA

A documentary format may be used for many nonfiction films that do not strictly adhere to using actuality materials. One might make a nonfiction film about Athens at its peak during ancient Greek times. This may be a combination of scholarly research, surveys of ancient ruins, and commentary combined with reenactments of certain events. As soon as reenactments are added, the format moves from a traditional educational documentary format to a partial nonfiction and fiction format since actors are being used to depict actions based on historical records or that are speculative. This technique is often called docudrama. However, at times it may become all drama and fiction.

BASED ON A TRUE STORY

The often-used term "Based on a True Story" must be categorized as fiction since it is scripted, uses actors, and is based on hearsay, first-person accounts, and information passed along and not witnessed or recorded by the filmmaker. However, one such film that does a great job of "being based on a true story" is The Thin Blue Line, directed by Errol Morris, which is often thought of as a documentary film but is a theatrical film using actors to reenact characters and events to create the story. Interviews with the subjects involved and dramatic recreations using actors to depict events are used. This type of presentation may be called a "docudrama." Thin Blue Line blends documentary actuality and theatrical speculation to reveal the story of a man convicted of a crime he allegedly did not commit. It has the look and feel of a documentary film.

A fine line exists between fiction and nonfiction when making documentary films. Sometimes, including what amounts to a fictional component of a documentary effort may be appropriate. For example, many historical documentary-style films and video productions include short segments using animation or actors, theatrical sets, or locations. These scenes, when carefully done, add a visual reality to the historical narrative. Since they are not "actuality" material, they are someone's impression of what may have happened, scripted, acted out, and therefore technically fiction. In certain instances, an animation may bring audio recordings to life.

Recorded Events

Recording an event like a football game without comment, editing, or narration does not make it a documentary. The event is recorded for archival purposes. We make a documentary film if we interview players, coaches, and others combined with some of that documentation, editing it into a story about the game. This is not to say that the archival footage of the game is objective, only that it has not been edited.

HYBRID DOCUMENTARIES

Many documentaries go beyond simply recording actuality. Filmmakers like Robert Flaherty feel that a subject involving real people needs to be preserved or explored, even though certain aspects of the story may be manipulated somehow. For example, Flaherty showed Nanook hunting using traditional methods in *Nanook of The North*. But the Inuit had already started using rifles for hunting, and the family Nanook was shown to be part of was not his family. What was staged was authentic but arranged by the filmmaker to take place. The actuality is accurate in that the event and people involved are not actors and are engaged in doing something they usually may do. The "fine line" between nonfiction and fiction may be an issue in this type of documentary.

HISTORICAL HYBRID DOCUMENTARIES

Documentaries with reenactments are a serious form of storytelling used for educational, informational, and entertainment purposes. While these programs are based on historical events, they may need to be more historically accurate since events are recreated. Historical writing is subjective. Historical Hybrid Documentaries should not be confused with Historical Dramas or "Period" films which are fictional dramatic narratives based on historical events or set in the past. While some aspects of the story may be "based" on historical fact, interpreting that reality is, by definition, theoretical and, therefore, considered subjective.

"MOCUMENTARY"

As the name implies, "mockumentaries" are satirical fictional, theatrical comedies, like Best In Show and This is Spinal Tap, that uses a faux documentary format. When done well, they are great entertainment but not documentaries or nonfiction.

"Attackumentary"

Some films and videos call themselves "documentaries" that are nothing more than thinly disguised propaganda, personal attacks, and character assassination vehicles. These videos do not attempt to discuss issues or explore reality. Instead, they conjure up bogus conspiracy theories, unsubstantiated facts, and outright lies to "attack" a person, institution, policy, or politician to bring them into question and harm them.

Stolen Honor is a character assassination attempt on Senator John Kerry, who is running for President of the United States. It is a fabricated story using mock interviews and footage edited in a documentary style. "Attackumentary" films are usually political and supported by political organizations with an ideology and political agenda. They go beyond ordinary propaganda in that they specialize in personal attacks. They are not documentaries.

Many documentaries, labeled "Advocacy," have a point of view that advocates an extreme position. While these films' narrow focus may border on propaganda, they may have credible sources and motives. They seek to find solutions to social and cultural problems. Advocacy documentaries are not "Attacking" anything. They are advocating ideas and causes. They look at what their point of view considers issues and offer solutions. There is a big difference between creating creditable nonfiction with an argument for or against an issue and creating a fictional, derogatory story about an individual or cultural institution.

Actualities

Lumière used the word "Actualities" for his films. The term "nonfiction" refers to everything that is not fiction. This covers a myriad of different types of projects. The most well-known type of nonfiction film or video is what is known as a documentary.

> *A documentary film is a story composed of "actuality" material. This could be film, video, photographs, first-person journals, or interviews on audio. The main factor in traditional documentary storytelling is that it spontaneously occurred and was not staged or recreated. In other words, it was recorded in some way when it happened.*

In his documentary about the American Civil War, Ken Burns introduces letters and journals written by soldiers in both armies. These are offered as first-hand accounts and recollections of those involved in the war. The documents have the perspectives of those individuals, and they are the authors. This kind of offering is considered the same as an interview or first-person account when not used out of context.

Other nonfiction genres may not necessarily be based on actuality but may deal with nonfiction subject matter. Nature films, Travel, Corporate, Industrial, Sales, Educational, and other topics fall into this category. They use a documentary style and incorporate actuality material and other instructional materials. These types of nonfiction films, videos, and multimedia projects will have detailed scripts that show what action is required.

A traditional-style documentary dealing with actuality usually takes the filmmaker out of the story. It isn't about the filmmaker. It's about the subject. But more recently, with the introduction of television documentaries that include the host narrator or reporter in the story, it is not unusual to find the filmmaker not only in front of the camera but also have the story centered around themselves. Films by Werner Herzog, Michael Moore, and others have adopted this format. They make the film about themselves and their experience or quest to explore a particular subject or issue. Films like *Supersize Me* have the filmmaker going through some trial or experience as the basis for the documentary. In *Supersize Me*, it was living on a fast-food diet for thirty days.

Documentaries by Herzog, Moore, and others tend to have the viewer experience everything through the filmmakers' eyes and points of view. It can feel like the films are really about them. Since they don't try to hide this fact, the films use a personal hybrid documentary format. This can be entertaining and informative. Many of these films have been successful theatrically at the Box Office. It could be argued that they fall within artistic expression and cinematic license. The question is, are they documentaries? Are they fiction or nonfiction?

For example, Werner Herzog uses strong music tracks and action footage in his films. *Into the Inferno* uses instrumental and choral singing (Unfailing Light Performed by the Monks Choir of Kyiv Pechersk Monastery and ten others) every time shots of active or inactive volcanoes are shown. At one point, a Requiem by Verdi is heard when two people go close to a lava flow. In this last case, the music foreshadows a tragic event. Why aren't the natural sounds of the volcanoes dramatic enough without what amounts to third-party commentary in the guise of Western classical music or opera? There wasn't an orchestra there at the volcano, even though Herzog may have heard one in his mind. In some cultures, volcanoes are treated as having spirits or religious significance. Perhaps, indigenous source music or natural sounds would allow the viewer to attach their feelings to the scene. The argument then goes to the role of the documentary filmmaker.

Is it to bring the viewer the actuality or to interpret it for the audience? Many viewers would like to experience the raw reality without someone else's subjective interpretation purposely interfering. Herzog believes, as an artist, that he represents the actuality to the audience. They come to see his art.

There are many approaches to making documentaries. But whatever the style, basic storytelling ideas are used to create a compelling story. Action, drama, conflict, and exciting characters make it possible to explore issues and subjects that audiences will want to watch.

Reviews and trailers for over a hundred fifty documentaries, including some highlighted or mentioned is this book, may be seen at: JRMartinMedia.com/ documentary-film-reviews

https://jrmartinmedia.com/

Documentary Production Crews must often work at the same time as other crews are shooting at large events.

Documentary Film Crews are often small working in all types of environments.

Heart of Shaolin documentary film crew working at Shaolin Temple in China.

"To the documentary director, the appearance of things and people is only superficial. It is the meaning behind the thing and the significance underlying the person that occupies his attention.

Documentary approach to cinema differs from that of story-film not in its disregard for craftsmanship, but in the purpose to which that craftsmanship is put.

Documentary is a trade, just as carpentry or pot-making. The pot-maker makes pots, and the documentarian documentaries."

—Paul Rotha

"My aim as a filmmaker is to approximate some of the complexity of the real world, rather than to simplify it" - Frederick Wiseman

Chapter 3

The Director and Preproduction

Developing and Researching Documentary and Nonfiction Projects

Ideas

Ideas are wonderful, but someone once said, "Ideas are a dime a dozen." It could be argued that documentary films and films generally are about more than ideas. They are about telling stories with a medium that is all about action and reaction. Ideas must come to life, not just be talked about or sound good on paper. It's one thing to have an idea for a documentary film; it is another to turn it into a story that others will understand or want to watch. What are the issues, questions, conflicts, and human realities involved? A director's job is to pre-visualize how the story will be told. This begins with the first shot in the film.

Pre-visualization

There are many ways to pre-visualize and structure a story, but all of them must be comprehensible to your audience. All stories have a beginning, middle, and end, whether fiction, nonfiction, or documentary. Documentary stories are a compilation of events, conversations, actions, reactions, and observations, including whatever conflict and tension naturally occur in the nonfiction material. The storyteller builds on these elements to tell the tale. In a documentary context, the storyteller may use existing conflict to tell the story without distorting the conflict to create false arguments or themes. As in all storytelling, from a joke to an epic novel, timing, structure, pacing, and delivery are essential. It is why two people can tell the same joke with opposite reactions.

The best stories engage the audience in a way that brings them into the process, allowing them to discover and ask questions (which, at some point, are answered) that evoke emotion. Questions to consider about an idea are, will it shed new light on the subject or topic? How interesting are the issues, and how long will it take to tell the story? How extensive is the topic? What is the focus of the exploration?

Audience

As difficult as it may be for the creative ego to accept, some ideas may have a different appeal. There may be only one person interested in a particular notion. Therefore, part of the research should be to see if anyone is interested in the subject being considered for production. Is there an audience for the subject large enough to support it? An educational film on a subject may be approached differently than a social advocacy documentary. They have different audiences. It is necessary to determine the demographics of the audience for the documentary. Some of this work can be done while researching the subject.

Research

The first step in developing the story is to research the subject by conducting preliminary talks with the people involved and studying the subject or topics for the documentary. Research helps develop an understanding of the subject and a focus for the story. Ultimately, interview questions can be based on what is learned in this phase. Go beyond what is known firsthand and discover what other sources say about the same subject. The most accessible place to start researching almost any subject or topic is to go online and "Google" it. There are other search engines available, as well. Read up on what information is found. Check Wikipedia. A social advocacy documentary may need to employ research techniques used by social scientists. A film looking into ecological issues in the Amazon or the impact of killer bees on North America will require consultants and some field research. Individuals who might be interviewed for the documentary may have fascinating histories or be well-known for their achievements. Research can give insight into their backgrounds and topics with which to launch your conversation. Begin the exploration with enough digging to know the current body of knowledge about the subject—all aspects, positive and negative, new and old. Explore with an open mind.

WHERE TO BEGIN RESEARCH

What has been written and discussed about the focus of the new documentary? Are there any documentaries already out there? Start the research by reading books and articles and screening other documentary or nonfiction works. Contact anyone who might have information or knowledge on the topic being researched. Do preliminary interviews with anyone knowledgeable or involved in the area of interest before filming. Make notes about issues or subjects that might contribute to the story. Explore other sources or experts the interviewee thinks are essential that substantiate or dispute their views. This process is similar to a journalist looking for facts and information to construct a story they are writing. In the case of a documentary, this is most often a story that will, in part, be told by the people involved. The research provides information about what questions to ask and how to approach the issues..

Exploring Reality

Documentaries are explorations of reality, not staged or manipulated situations. Refrain from going into making a documentary with the notion that the answers to the questions are already known or personally trying to push specific ideas. A better way to explore is to ask questions to learn something new. Like a child, listen to the answers without judgment. Children learn by asking questions as they explore the world growing up. Young children don't go out with preconceived notions of what they will find. They ask out of curiosity, genuinely wanting to learn about the world and how they fit in.

Starting a documentary without firm pre-conceived ideas about someone or something facilitates discovery. It may be found that what was thought would happen, what was imagined about a subject, or what a place might be like, is different. Never encountering or acknowledging new realities might indicate a problem in perception. There is a need to go beyond the superficial, contrived situations and seek to understand the facts being explored. Keep an inquisitive attitude while researching and making the documentary.

It may be that an individual or group has an idea for a documentary about a controversial topic. There is a personal point-of-view about that particular subject. Someone feels motivated to tell a story that doesn't appear to be getting related. Perhaps they want to promote some idea, movement, or institution. This can be done in a documentary format, but it may end up as propaganda, presented as a documentary. Research and investigation into opposing ideas on a given issue are essential. If you are asked to direct this type of documentary project, you must know what the producers expect to do with the documentary. Who is the audience? What is the message? It would be best to have a firm grip on the story to be told.

Many groups talk about "alternative realities." However, their personal or group reality may not meet the objective reality test of being proven factually true or false. This is despite facts and coverage coming from multiple independent sources. Particular print, television, and broadcast entities with political agendas distort realities to suit their ideologies. They change their opinions and facts depending on to whom they present them. Lobby groups also push alternative conclusions about events, subjects, and people involved distorting the reality for their purposes. In this day and age of the Internet, individuals, institutions, political groups, lobbyists, corporations, and governments (foreign and domestic) can all instantly voice their opinions to the world. These opinions are often highly subjective. Documentaries based on this type of information are likely candidates as propaganda. When you commit to a project, understand the priorities.

FIND THE STORY

Is there a story here? What is that story, and how will the story be told? An excellent way to start finding if there is a story is to create an outline of issues, main characters, or where it is thought the story might go. List the issues, individuals, and other information uncovered in the research. Look for those elements, beginning, middle, and end, that may form the basis for the story. Imagine what the first shot or scene is in the documentary.

After all the research, it comes down to finding the most critical aspects of the documentary story.

Assessing An Idea For A Documentary Film

Check List

Who is the audience for this documentary?
How will this idea or issue be turned it in to a story with a beginning, middle, and end?
What is the first shot in the story?
What will be seen on the screen beside interviews?
What is the action on the screen?
What questions will be asked?
What kind of research has been conducted on this idea?
Have there been other films on this subject?
What did the other films cover?
How will this film be different?
What exactly will be documented?
Who is the protagonist, and who is the antagonist in this story?
What is the conflict?
Write a concept, treatment, shooting script and story-board.
What type of coverage will be shot?
What film festival featuring, or accepting documentaries do you think would be interested in this film?
What category or area would this documentary be listed under, social, historical, political, anthropological, etcetera?
Will anyone beside a few friends want to view this documentary? Why?

Consultants

During the research and writing stage, it's a good idea to find consultants or experts knowledgeable about the issues involved in the documentary. They may be academics who are experts in a related field. For example, a documentary about immigration might want to consult with a historian and a sociologist who has written about this subject. Social workers and others who deal with immigrants could provide additional insight. The appropriate government agency may provide information on policy subject to current politics

Writing a Concept and Treatment

Concept

Conceptualize the story into a brief sentence or two. This is not always an easy task, but a worthwhile one for the director and is a way to convey succinctly to others what the story is about or where it will go.

Treatment

A documentary film treatment should be short, about two pages for a feature-length documentary. This is not a script. A treatment is a summary of how the subject will be approached, and it should generally elaborate on the concept. The treatment shows where the story will go beginning, middle, and end. Necessary to include in the treatment are the issues that will be explored and a sample of what questions will be asked. The treatment must give the reader a sense of who, what, when, why, where, and how. Written well, it can help build interest in the documentary.

Treatments for longer documentary projects may be more than a couple of pages. Additional pages can discuss other concerns depending on who will read them. For example, a treatment meant to "pitch" or sell the idea might include more information on why this is an important, topical subject and why making the film is essential. This "pitch" section can supplement the original two pages without being integrated with the story treatment. The story treatment is a narrative. Ideally, it must hold the readers' attention and bring them into the story—no commercials during the narrative.

The concept and treatment grow from an initial idea, research, outline, or breakdown of the subject areas. It forms the basis for the story, a script, and a shooting script. The treatment should convey the filmmaker's knowledge of the subject. A treatment that gives a strong notion of the envisioned documentary can be presented on paper or in other forms, including a film or video trailer, photographic portfolio, audio program, or slide presentation. A well-thought-out concept and treatment provide a place to begin, bringing the idea to life.

SHOOTING SCRIPT PREPARATION

After the concept and treatment are finalized, the director writes a shooting script in collaboration with a writer or on their own. Usually, a shooting script is not written until the project is "green-lighted" and a preliminary budget is approved. Under most circumstances, the shooting script is the basis for gathering the footage necessary to tell the intended story. Sometimes a shooting script is more of a wish list, but it does provide a framework for getting the coverage needed to tell the story. *The shooting script does not detail what the subject will do or say. The shooting script provides a plan for what to shoot to tell the story proposed in the concept and treatment. The shooting script is a plan to obtain adequate coverage to tell the story.*

This plan may change depending on the circumstances. However, it is a place to start rather than beginning with a vague notion of shooting something or following someone around to see what happens. The director's job is to get the shots and interviews that can be edited to depict whatever story is proposed. A documentary director must think about how the scene will be edited while shooting the scene. This means getting shots that cut together. It's the director's responsibility, but the camera operator should also know the need for various cutaways and different size shots, especially during an interview. The director and camera operator should discuss the coverage the director is looking for. The camera operator must think and listen to what is happening while shooting.

Writing The Shooting Script

A shooting script for a documentary does not "script" what the subject will do or say. It details what the filmmakers will do and the questions that will be asked. In some cases where there will be a voice-over narrator, the script will show what the narration might be and the picture that goes with it. But this narration may change in the final editing script once the footage has been obtained. First-person interviews will be used in certain scenes instead of the voice-over narrator.

The shooting script for a documentary is a guide to shooting, a wish list in some ways, for action that fits the vision for that scene. Some scripted images may not be obtainable, while other opportunities might present themselves as shooting progresses. The shooting script is the basis for getting the coverage necessary to tell the story. It is also needed to determine the equipment and crew required for scheduling and budget considerations.

Formats for nonfiction film scripts and documentaries differ from those for theatrical fiction film screenplays. A basic two-column script with a column for the picture and a column for the audio is used. A column for the shot number and one for the approximate time of the shot may be added. This format works as a shooting script or an editing script. It sometimes has another column in nonfiction production for a storyboard picture or photograph.

Documentary films explore actuality, events that spontaneously happen over which little control exists. It may not seem practical to write a formal shooting script. But there must be a basic plan to cover these unpredictable events. Where will the camera or cameras be placed? An essential asset is a shooting script that shows what questions will be asked, what shots, and how you intend to structure the coverage.

Sometimes a simple shot list and list of questions may be adequate to help insure getting some archival coverage of a one-time event that will be part of a larger project. Certain nonfiction films, videos, or multimedia projects require a script since these stories are predictable. They may employ both nonfiction and fictional resources. In a pure documentary shooting script, describe the shots desired, who will be interviewed, questions, photographs, quotes, and other necessary information.

A story that combines actuality-style material or archival footage with dramatized recreations or anything that uses actors instead of real people falls into a gray area that is both nonfiction and fiction. If theatrical segments are used in a documentary, they are treated as fictional scenes and scripted in a screenplay format. A multi-column script is appropriate for a compilation documentary that uses archival footage, photographs, interviews, and other actuality-based material. A shooting script for a documentary project shows what shots and questions are pre-visualized for telling the story. The script might say to get "coverage" of certain aspects of the event and interviews with whoever might be necessary. If circumstances change, it is still the director's job to get the shots and interviews that can be edited together and used in the documentary. The director must think about how the scene will be edited while shooting. This requires the ability to pre-visualize the edited shots in their head while shooting.

For example, a person essential to the documentary story is interviewed. It is necessary, if possible, to get footage of what they're talking about ("B" roll) along with general coverage (action) of the event. It's the director's responsibility, but the camera operator should also know the need for various cutaways and different size shots during an interview. The director and camera operator discuss the kind of coverage the director seeks. During shooting, the camera operator is alert, listening, and following the action.

In preproduction, break down the shooting script into which shots will be shot at each camera setup. For example, questions may be asked in a different order than in the shooting script, using a particular camera setup to save time. It may be necessary to shoot shots out of script order to avoid moving the camera and lights multiple times. This saves time and helps ensure continuity in lighting and camera angles.

Finally, the questions in the shooting script are a place to start. New questions will come to mind as one listens to the interviewee. Follow up on these questions because they can be more revealing than the ones scripted before the shoot. Listen to the interviewee's answers. Try to have a short conversation with the interviewee rather than asking a list of formal questions. An interview may evolve as the conversation proceeds.

One of the main ideas for creating a shooting script is to ensure adequate coverage for editing. Whenever possible, visit the location before writing the shooting script. For example, a documentary about a restaurant owner, shot on location, in the restaurant, can be researched by visits to the restaurant before shooting. A shooting script can be written detailing coverage of the staff, the kitchen, and what questions will be asked if the interviews are done simultaneously. Planning coverage allows for more options during the editing process.

A shooting and editing script for a documentary or nonfiction project looks similar. They both use a multiple-column format beginning with two columns, one for picture and one for audio. Additional columns may be added for storyboards or other information. The page can be in portrait or landscape mode. In our example, two columns are added—a column for the shot number and another for the length of the shot (time). Sometimes, a detailed shooting script can't be written because it isn't known exactly what will happen. A shooting script based on a wish list of coverage or a shot list of various shots and angles for the action and interviews can still be written. After the shoot, the footage is logged, and an editing script based on the actual footage is written. The editing script is written to provide the editor and director with a guide to structure the story using the footage available. How the story is ultimately edited may change as the postproduction process evolves. The postproduction process is covered in Chapter 5.

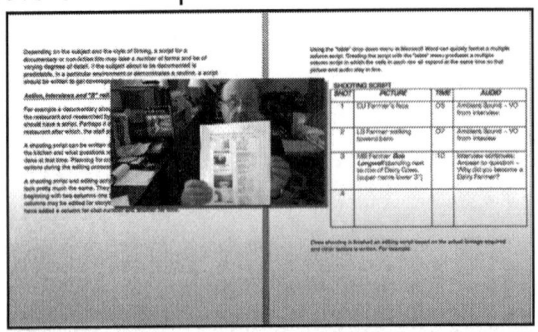

Short video on formatting a multi-column script for a documentary. See page 141.

SHOOTING SCRIPT

SHOT	PICTURE	TIME	AUDIO
1	CU Farmer's face	:05	Ambient Sound - VO from interview.
2	LS Farmer walking toward barn	:07	Ambient Sound - VO from inteview
3	MS Farmer **Bob Longwell** standing next to row of Dairy Cows. (super name lower 3")	:10	Interview continues: Answer to question - Why did you become a Dairy Farmer?
4			

How to Format a Multi-column Shooting or Editing Script

The multi-column script format may be used for any documentary or nonfiction project. This includes industrial, corporate, educational, sales, commercial, informational film, video, or multimedia projects. Using the "landscape" rather than "portrait" layout allows for additional columns to be added for the storyboard or other information.

Include the event activities and the subject's actions in the script if they are predictable. Include any details known about the environment or action.

A multi-column script is formatted using the "table" drop-down menu in Microsoft Word®. Creating the script with the "table" menu produces a multiple-column script in which the cells in each row expand simultaneously so that Picture and Audio frames stay next to each other in the same row.

Pick the number of columns (four) and rows (around ten rows would be plenty) ten is good. More rows can always be added by tabbing on the last cell to add another row. Size your columns by dragging the lines to where you want them.

EDITING SCRIPT

SHOT	PICTURE	TIME	AUDIO
1	CU Farmer's face	:05	Ambient Sound – VO from interview. *"Well I never really thought about it, my Father was a Dairy Farmer and so was his Father..."*
2	LS Farmer walking toward barn	:07	Ambient Sound – VO from interview. *...I guess it just runs in the family.*
2A	CU of Tractor	:03	Ambient sound Farmer walking
2B	CU Farmer opening gate	:04	Ambient sound gate opening
3	MS Farmer **Bob Longwell** standing next to row of Dairy Cows. (super name lower 3")	:10	Interview continues: Answer to question – Why did you become a Dairy Farmer? *...we have 100 cows at this time...*
4			

The great thing about the table format is that it keeps the cells in each row lined up as the information is added to a cell, so your Picture and Audio frames stay opposite.

Professional audio-visual script writing software programs like Final Draft® AV are available, which align with budgeting and other Final Draft® software.

Once shooting is finished, an editing script based on the footage acquired is written. However, cutaways might be added to supplement a shot like the Farmer walking toward the barn.

For a short video on formatting a multicolumn script using Microsoft Word® go to: https://www.youtube.com/watch?v=vCApfQOglZs&t=66s

http://www.jrmartinmedia.com/book/writing-a-shooting-script-and-editing-script-for-documentary-film-or-non-fiction-project/

Copyright

As early as the scripting stage, thought should be given to possible copyright issues. Copyright laws give the owner the exclusive copyright use of the copyrighted work. Anyone wishing to use any portion of that work must have the copyright holder's permission. There are no exceptions. Over time there has grown a grey area called "fair use." Fair use covers certain situations or circumstances where protected work may be permitted. There are no fair use laws. The concept of fair use is a defense; that something owned by someone else is being used without obtaining permission because you feel it doesn't infringe on the other person's copyright, trademark, or likeness in a way that violates the spirit of copyright protection. Since there are no fair use laws, one can only make a case that using the protected work in a particular way does not infringe on the copyright. Some "rules of thumb" may be used to gauge fair use.

Rules of Thumb to consider before using copyrighted material.

What is Fair Use of Copyrighted Material?

Is the work protected? Since 1989 absence of a copyright notice does not necessarily mean the work is not protected.

Is the work original? Compilations, like the phone book, are facts and are not able to be copyrighted.

Is the work in public domain? Generally, work published before December 31, 1922 is considered public domain.

USA citizens may use work created by the US Government.

Ideas, processes, methods, and systems described in copyrighted work cannot be copyrighted.

The use of quotes, or short segments from copyrighted work in scholarly publications, newspaper articles, books, documentary films, educational work, critical reviews, and satirical parodies is usually considered fair use.

The above list is not intended as legal advice. It is only offered as a layman's guide to the gray area known as "Fair Use." Legal counsel should be consulted.

Highly recommended for a detailed discussion of intellectual property law is, *The Pocket Lawyer for Filmmakers by Thomas A. Crowell, Esq. Focal Press, 2007.* According to Mr. Crowell, there are many factors a court considers when determining fair use. These factors include *"the purpose and character of the use," "the nature of the copyrighted work," "the amount of the portion of copyrighted work used,"* and *"how the use of the work influences the potential market or value of the copyrighted work."* While these are valid factors to consider before using copyrighted material, they are no guarantee that there will not be other considerations.

Many fair use areas apply to educational applications by teachers and students, as long as the use is academic and not commercial. It should be noted that whether or not a profit is made does not determine fair use.

Archival photographs, film, or video clips in documentary films follow the same guidelines as those for print. Stock footage libraries base their rates on educational, commercial, and theatrical uses.

DIRECTOR AND PRODUCER

There are many responsibilities a director should be familiar with concerning preproduction. Once a project becomes "Green Lighted," given the go-ahead, development work is finalized. The producer of the project manages preproduction. The director is involved in this process with the producer and others.

If a producer is involved, they most likely hire the director because they feel they are the right person to direct the production. The director should understand the concept of the documentary and be able to pre-visualize a look and feel for how the story will appear on the screen. Directors tend to specialize in certain types of documentaries. Someone who directs educational films will be considered to direct other educational projects. A director is hired to work a set number of weeks in preproduction, production, and postproduction. The exception, of course, is if the director is working as a Producer/Director/Writer (Filmmaker) on a project.

The director's preproduction responsibilities include finalizing the shooting schedule and coordinating plans with the Director of Photography (DP) and other crew members. Depending on the size and scope of the project, a first assistant director and script supervisor are hired. They will work closely with the director during the project.

The project's producer is the person who handles the budget and hiring of key "above-the-line" staff, like the director. Often, a documentary project's producer, director, and writer are the same person. If so, some assistance is needed for help in these areas. Depending on the project's scope, an associate producer or assistant producer, first assistant director, and perhaps another writer.

Production of a documentary or some nonfiction project follows much the same pattern as a fiction film. The first step is to break down the shooting script to see what is needed to produce the documentary. This includes estimating how long it will take to shoot, the crew required, and the equipment needed, among many other things.

Shooting Script Breakdown

The first thing to do when breaking down a documentary shooting script is to look at locations. Next, what needs to be shot at each location, how many days it will take, what size crew, and what equipment and other resources are required. At each location, how many camera setups will be required? If possible, schedule all the shots included in the script, wherever in the script they occur, at the same time for each setup. It's necessary to determine how many camera setups will be required because it will take time to set up and light each time the camera is moved. Some documentary situations will be very fluid. The camera or cameras will need to follow the action. Setups may be using available light because they can't be lit for some reason. The director should discuss the coverage they seek in that situation with the camera department.

Next, look at transportation requirements. Some documentaries may require going back to the exact location several times. Is this a one-time event being covered, or will a series of one-time events be part of this documentary? If so, over what period will they occur?

Particularly important to documentary filmmaking is obtaining firm location permits and agreements from anyone who will be interviewed. Access to the location, venue, or event may be verbal or written. But some written agreement or pass must be obtained for significant public events. A talent release with each interviewee is signed before the interview takes place. This release gives the production permission to use the interview in the film. There are standard release forms available online. Location releases are signed by the property owner where the shooting occurs. Some property owners will require liability insurance to cover any damage that might happen. Production companies carry workman's compensation and liability insurance. Film and video production rental houses also need insurance to rent equipment.

If a documentary is being produced for theatrical release shooting using film stock may be justified. The process would be to shoot using film, then transfer it to a digital format for editing. However, today with high-end digital formats available, it is unlikely that shooting on film can be justified cost-wise. Considerations are quality and expense. Is this project for the big screen, television screen, or the Internet? Today high-end "4k" and "8k" digital formats can be released theatrically. Very few films are released to theaters in an analog format now.

After breaking down the script and estimating the number of days and locations, it is time to look at crew and equipment needs. At this time, the producer gets together with the director and the director of photography (DP) to review the shooting script, breakdown, and location schedule. The DP reviews the coverage the director wants to get and suggests what equipment and lights will be required. The producer or an assistant makes calls to confirm locations and get agreements from the documentary's subjects. The director and the DP will scout locations.

Choosing a Crew

As was mentioned earlier, the director often gets to pick the cinematographer of their choice. This could be someone they have worked with before. It would be typical for the DP to be the camera operator in a documentary crew. Their lighting and shooting style should be compatible with the director's vision and requirements. There needs to be a high level of communication between the director and the DP/Camera Operator. The DP usually chooses their assistants and camera/audio crew. The Director may also select or recommend the First Assistant Director and the Script Supervisor. From a team standpoint, the director works closest with the DP/Operator, Script Supervisor, and First Assistant Director.

Not all of the following positions are required for documentary projects. The size of the crew depends on the scope of the project and budget.

Basic Documentary Film Crew -- Key job descriptions:

Writer

The writer in a documentary production may be the same person as the director and the producer. A writer may be employed in a nonfiction production for an educational film, a corporate training film, or a television-style documentary production. Depending on the needs of the production, they may be asked to research and find archival and historical records to develop a script for narration. Writers may be asked to work with the producer and director to maintain historical accuracy concerning events and dialogue.

First Assistant Director (AD)

The first AD performs many administrative duties for the director, including scheduling shooting, arranging logistics, calling personnel to the proper location for shooting, maintaining order on the set or location, checking budgets, and communicating with department heads. He or she ensures that all proposed or planned shots are completed. In small crews, the first AD and script supervisor positions may be combined.

Script Supervisor

Script supervisors are responsible for maintaining a record of individual takes and details, including the beginning and end of takes; their durations; the properties appearing in the shot; the camera's position and movement; and an example or synopsis of the dialogue recorded. They help bridge complementary ideas and images from scene to scene and ensure that all proposed or planned shots are covered and all impromptu ones are logged. In a documentary, the script supervisor may absorb some of the second assistant cameraperson's responsibilities regarding helping with logs. Sometimes, they may also serve as the video assist technician/VTR and first assistant director.

Director of Photography (DP)

The director of photography on a documentary film works closely with the director and the camera operator. The DP is responsible for lighting a given location to get good exposure and to enhance the lighting of a given location's overall look and feel. The DP may operate portable lighting devices during shooting. The DP sets up the general composition of the scene, chooses cameras, lenses, filters, camera settings, movements, and integration of any special effects, animation, or optical effects. Depending on the production size, the camera crew may include a gaffer for lighting and grip assistants.

Gaffer

The gaffer is responsible for placing, operating, and maintaining the required lights and their power sources for illumination in studio and location environments. They oversee general power requirements for all equipment, including the all-important battery supplies. With the DP, he may be asked to scout locations to determine power requirements, existing lighting availability, and location weather conditions. The best boy is an assistant to the Gaffer. The best boy helps rig lighting and keeps track of lighting costs.

Camera Operator

The camera operator works with the Director of Photography and is directly responsible for managing the camera during shooting. If there are two cameras, there will be two camera operators. The camera operator views the scene through the viewfinder, ensuring the image is composed and focused correctly. They adjust settings and camera positioning. The camera operator performs camera movements and static compositions and should be familiar with locations before the shoot, if possible. Experience with handheld camera work, camera-assist units (e.g., Steadicam, jibs), and ENG style are essential. This position may be combined with the Director of Photography.

Grips

Grips perform various duties, including transporting and setting up equipment, especially lighting accessories, moving, placing props, and scenery, setting dolly tracks, and operating dollies. He or she answers to the art director, the director of photography, or the camera operator and may work as an operator for crane or jib equipment. Said by some are named "Grips" because they need to maintain a firm "grip" while carrying objects or pushing/pulling the dolly.

Sound Mixer

Sound mixers are responsible for recording sound and mixing audio levels during a shooting in a clear, accurate, balanced manner. They must be familiar with a wide array of recording instruments, unique polar patterns, construction, area acoustics, and local ambiance. The sound mixer maintains recording equipment, sound logs/reports, notes any necessary sound effects, room tone, or ambiance, and supervises this position. The sound mixer works with a boom operator or may do that job as well.

Boom Operator

The boom operator maintains the boom pole or fish pole so that the attached microphone is always pointed at the appropriate subject to pick up the best recording consistent with said microphone's particular polar pattern. A boom operator strives not to interfere with the visual aspects of the production. In other words, keeps the boom and microphone out of the shot. The boom operator wears a headset to monitor the audio from the microphone on the boom pole.

Editor

The editor shapes and arranges shots, scenes, and sequences while modulating and integrating sound and music to bring rhythm, mood, tone, emphasis, and story to the final impact of the piece. The editor incorporates graphics, on-screen titles, animated sequences, stills, and stock footage where appropriate. The editor works closely with the director to create the pacing and feel desired by the director. The director supervises the film's first cut as the director's vision is being edited.

Production Assistants (PA

PA's generally work with specific department heads and perform a variety of important tasks for the production, including distribution and posting of printed materials, preparation for shooting, crowd control, office duties (making copies and answering phones), and running general errands ("go for" food or last-minute supplies). Production Assistants work with all other positions.

Depending on production priorities and budget, additional traditional film production positions may be required.

PRODUCER

The documentary producer may generate original concepts or purchase, adapt, or handle existing ideas and scripts from other sources. The producer puts the production together from inception and sees it through to distribution. There are several different types of producers. An executive producer is usually someone associated with the project's financing or the production company's head. A producer may be employed by the production company or hired as an independent producer for a specific project. Independent producers may also originate projects independently and find financing for those projects. A line producer is someone who works for another producer. The line producer supervises projects in the same way the producer does.

Producers secure financing, make production, distribution, and exhibition deals for the project, and hire the director and other crew members as necessary. The producer's staff oversees location scouting, scheduling, budgeting, travel arrangements for the crew, talent (if any), and interviewees. In an auteur filmmaker situation, the producer may be the writer, director, interviewer, and editor. Producers oversee payroll and petty cash.

It should be noted that many types of projects fall under the nonfiction category and are different from traditional actuality-based documentary efforts. These nonfiction projects include training films, historical reenactments, docudramas, and educational, scientific, and so-called "reality-based" television programming. The producer's role will vary depending on the type of project. Other members of the producer's category are the unit manager or a production manager, who helps coordinate a project and report to the producer

PREPRODUCTION CHECK LIST

Ideas and approach finalized.	Producer, Director, Writer
Research on subject and related topics conducted.	Director and Writer
Concept and Treatment Written.	Director, Writer and Producer
Financing secured, Budget	Producer
Agreements signed. Releases obtained.	Producer
Shooting Script written. Questions for Interviews discussed. Additional Research as required.	Director, Director of Photography, Writer
Locations visited if possible.	Director, Director of Photography
Break down Shooting Script Locations, Events, Interviews	Director, Producer
Dates for shooting confirmed.	Producer, Director, 1st AD
Crew hired, dates working confirmed.	Producer, Director, 1st AD
Equipment and material resources needed confirmed and obtained for shooting dates.	Producer, Director, Director of Photography, Sound Mixer, Gaffer.
Location accommodations and meals confirmed.	Producer, 1st AD, Staff

Transportation and Per Diem (travel away from home base) ready for location crew.	Producer, Staff
Budget Finalized.	Producer
Call times, transportation set for everyone.	1st AD
Final confirmation with interview subjects, locations dates and times.	Producer, Director, Staff
Release Forms, Location permits, and releases confirmed.	Producer, Director, Staff
Equipment check.	Director of Photography, Camera operator, Sound Mixer, Gaffer
Transportation, catering arranged for crew.	Producer, Staff
Transportation of equipment.	Camera and Grip department

Wrapped In Steel Documentary Film Crew. Shooting 16mm film in Southeast Chicago.

COVERAGE

In a documentary context getting coverage begins with the idea that enough footage will be shot of a particular event, action, or location to allow an editor to reconstruct the scene seamlessly. Shooting the main activity at an event must include a way for the editor to edit the event without awkward-cutting choices. This means a variety of shots of the main action and additional coverage known as the "B" roll. This "B" roll is footage that can be used to help edit the story. For example, an interview is done in someone's office. "B" roll is shots of the office, framed pictures, awards, or other things in that office. Perhaps something outside the office that is mentioned in the interview. Getting adequate coverage in a documentary situation is the responsibility of the director.

Chapter 4

The Director and Production

The director will have some long days during production. Early meetings and late wraps are usual. The director greatly relies on the DP/Operator, First Assistant Director, and Script Supervisor during production.

The producer or production manager is involved in the handling of logistics for the director. The director needs to focus on getting the shots and coverage of what's happening that day in context with how it will be used to tell the story. The less the director has to think about logistics like transportation, meals, etcetera, the better. Budgets for documentary films are often reasonably tight, so crews and support staff are small. The filmmakers may wear more than one hat, and specific crew positions may be combined. For example, a first AD may be a production manager and script supervisor. The director becomes "the captain of the ship" of production. They need whatever support is available. The director earns that support by creating a team spirit and a good working environment. At the same time, the crew must behave professionally and be supportive under all circumstances.

After all the preparation, the director's job of gathering the footage or coverage that will be used to construct the documentary story begins. A documentary director must be well prepared with a vision of the look and feel of how the story will be told. To start with, what kind of lighting will be used in the documentary? Will available light only be used? Available light augmented with fill? Will the interviews be lit in a certain way? Additional lighting of events or subjects in a documentary can change the story's reality and give it an artificial feel. Working with the director of photography, the director discusses their priorities and the desired lighting look.

Lighting documentaries is a tricky proposition. Theoretically, the lighting should not alter the actuality. Augmenting the available light to help camera exposure is the task at hand. However, this additional lighting can support the available light look and feel. In some situations, it is impossible to light an entire space—for example, covering a large rally in a hall lit with fluorescent lights. Even if the hall cannot be lit, rigging a few lights on the podium where the speakers will address the audience may be possible. Lighting situations will be covered in more detail later in this chapter.

The DP's first question for the director is where do you want the camera? The next thing the director will discuss with the DP/Camera Operator is the lens type and size of shots. The DP/Camera Operator needs to know what kind of shot the director wants. Is it a close-up with limited depth of field or a wide shot? What is to be seen in the picture?

In today's high-end digital video production world, the director, DP/Operator, audio mixer, and script supervisor can view and listen to what has been shot on the fly and review what has been covered at the end of the day. It is the director's responsibility to look through the camera lens at times, before the shot, often at the invitation of the camera operator. With video assistance, the director and others can see what is being shot as it is recorded. But many directors like to keep their attention focused on the live action. The video assist operator can alert someone of problems. Listening to recorded audio with the video is also a good idea. The director may communicate with the camera operator through a wireless headset.

An experienced director has already constructed scenes in their mind or on a storyboard about the type of shots they want to cover a scene. In a documentary situation, it is only sometimes possible to know what the location will look like beforehand. Some reasonably standard approaches may be customized to the director's priorities and style. Ideas for coverage may arise spontaneously once on location.

For example, suppose there is an outdoor event in a park. It's a good idea to establish the park setting. There could be one wide shot or a series of shots that establish the park. These could be static shots or moving images. Maybe a drone shot of the entire venue, followed by tighter shots of specific people or areas. Close-ups are shot to highlight details about the environment. Was there a sign at the entrance of the park? It might be worth getting a shot of it, along with people passing by. All of this with continuity of screen direction and location integrity and continuity.

Once again, it is the director's responsibility to get enough coverage to enable the editor, in postproduction, to construct the scene in a way that recreates the actuality that was there. The director's choices in each situation will give the documentary a look and feel. The DP/camera operator and the director must be on the same page. If there are multiple cameras, it should be clear what coverage and shots each camera is responsible for. Footage from each camera must match in terms of lighting, camera angles, and shot sizes. All coverage must be complementary for editing purposes.

In a studio situation, camera operators get instructions via headphones. The technical director can watch monitors for each camera. A documentary director may need help communicating directly with the second or third camera operator on location. Each camera operator needs an assignment of what to shoot. In some situations, there may be a need for a second unit director, camera operator, and audio mixer. The DP or 1st AD can coordinate coverage with the additional camera crew.

The director's talent and experience are essential in the production phase of making a documentary. Responsibilities extend beyond leading the crew. The director's interaction with the subjects and people involved will set the tone for cooperation and spontaneity. Every director brings their personality into the equation. Each situation may require a slightly different approach by the director. There should be mutual respect between members of the crew and the director.

DOCUMENTARY PRODUCTION

There are significant differences between directing a documentary production versus directing methods for television programming and newsgathering. Electronic News Gathering (ENG) production relies mainly on handheld shots of newscasters in the field, panoramic views of events, and a few attempts at visual storytelling. Available lighting is standard, with the occasional camera-mounted light used as fill light or to pierce the darkness for proper exposure. ENG camera operators are talented and often sent out independently to get coverage or "B" roll footage.

Documentary film storytelling is based on cinematic conventions and methods employing the composition of shots, lenses, tripods, dolly and track, lighting, and editing styles found in most fiction films. Introducing electronic recording devices and high-definition digital video instead of filmstock does not change production methodology. It only changes the recording medium. This is not to say that recording images electronically rather than on filmstock does not change the look and feel of what is shot. On the contrary, it has dramatically changed what is seen and felt on the screen. Even though filmstock is rarely used now for documentary work, it is vital to understand the differences between film and digital.

The characteristics of the medium being used are essential to understand. For example, video has less depth of field than film. Inherently video is less engaging than film. Be familiar with electronic media characteristics. In documentary filmmaking, lighting helps create the texture, the colors, and how the audience will react to each shot and scene. The director might choose lighting that alters the color saturation and the mood of the scene or interview. This is a delicate process since subjective lighting may change the reality of what is being shot.

Marshal McLuhan said, "The Medium is the Message." In short, he claims that the medium used to convey the information influences the perception of the transmitted data. The analog images seen on film differ from the electronic images seen on television. Film is considered a "hot" medium, and television (video) is a "cool" medium. Filmstock is a celluloid material that records light onto its surface, making frames of small transparent photographs. When the film is projected, light shines through the film producing an image on the screen. This warm light image engages the viewer. Other hot media are paper and money, which also present tangible images that engage us.

Television's electronically produced video image is considered a "cool" medium. Essentially a digital, LCD, or electronic screen device on which are projected lines and fields with electronic coolness. This does not evoke the emotional reaction that an analog film in a theater does because it lacks detail. Television electronically projects points of light that form an illusion of an image. Films shot digitally that will be screened in theaters are high definition and processed for a big screen. Some digital formats now have higher resolution than 35 mm film. But the analog tactile qualities are missing along with the warmth.

Hot media, usually but only sometimes, facilitate complete involvement without considerable stimulus. For example, print occupies visual space, uses visual senses, and immerses the reader. Hot media favor analytical precision, quantitative analysis, and sequential ordering, as they are usually sequential, linear, and logical. They emphasize one sense (for example, sight or sound) over the others. For this reason, hot media also include radio, film, live lectures, and photography. Cool media provide less direct stimulus. They require more active participation on the user's part, including the perception of abstract patterning and simultaneous comprehension of all aspects. McLuhan describes the term "cool media" as emerging from jazz and popular music and, in this context, is used to mean "detached.

In 2018, theatrical films worldwide began being released on hard drives to the theaters for transfer and projection on DCI-standardized Digital Cinema[1] projectors. Audiences no longer know how analog film projection looks and feels. There is a difference. Ever notice how easy it is to fall asleep watching television? Although some may blame it on the quality of theatrical films, the same tendency is becoming apparent in movie theaters, where it was previously rare.

Creating a documentary for theatrical release differs from making a documentary for television. Television needs more close-ups and action than a big theatrical screen to tell a story. Cutting is generally faster for TV. Shooting on film, to ultimately show on television, must consider that the images will be seen on a smaller screen than in most theaters. Also, when shooting wide-screen or high-definition formats, consider that not everyone has a wide-screen television and that most action must happen within standard TV-safe areas. Today homes have large-screen televisions, and theaters have even larger screen digital projection. It's all digital now. Theatrical release films need more action, tighter shots, and fast-paced editing to keep people awake in the theater.

1 https://en.wikipedia.org/wiki/Digital_cinema#Projectors_for_digital_cinema

Types of Scenes

There are three types of scenes a director may encounter. First, action with no dialogue. Second, dialogue with no action. Third, action and dialogue. Each type of scene requires a different type of coverage.

Action no Dialogue

A parade is all action and no dialogue. Standard practice is to shoot a master shot, reasonably wide, of the parade coming toward the viewer. Additionally, close-ups of individual band members or marchers as insert shots to be used with the master shot. Also needed are MSs and CUs of the people watching the parade. Are there floats? Include a Longshot (LS) of the floats, and CUs of people on the floats are good. The band's audio and the scene's ambient sound should be recorded. Another aspect of coverage is the screen direction of the marchers. Usually, moving from the screen left to the screen right implies the parade is coming toward us, passing, then moving away from us. Moving from the screen right to the screen left may indicate a change in screen direction or make it appear the marchers have reversed direction. Screen direction continuity is essential so as not to confuse the viewer.

Dialogue no Action

Also known as "talking heads." Good coverage includes camera movement and different size shots to provide editing choices and ways to cut out the questions asked. A scene might start with a Full Shot (FS) of the interviewee standing or sitting. The interviewer asks the interviewee to introduce themself. The camera operator frames a MS to cover this dialogue. While the interviewer asks the next question, the camera operator pushes in and frames a CU. Each time a question is asked, the camera operator changes the size of the shot. This gives the editor some choices and is much better than the camera locked off in a static MS for the entire interview. An alert camera operator might find times when pushing in or pulling back while the interviewee answers give the shot some impact. For example, the shot can be tighter if the interviewee becomes emotional. Shots can be wider if the interviewee becomes animated by moving arms around. Camera operators should not lock off the camera during an interview. They must be alert, keep the subject in the frame, and be ready to make subtle adjustments for changing circumstances.

ACTION AND DIALOGUE

A political rally situation has both action and dialogue and requires an assortment of shots of people moving around, signs, posters, and images of speakers. This might start as all action and end up as action and dialogue if interviews with the people attending the rally are included. There is a need to consider the movement of people in the scene, at the location, and who should be covered. Conversations between people at the event can be shot from an internal point of view or externally, as an outside observer in a Direct Cinema context.

FOCAL LENGTH OF LENS

It is crucial to consider the focal length of the lens being used. A wide-angle lens will give increased depth of field. A telephoto lens will decrease the depth of field. The camera's position and height relative to the subject are essential to recording the interview or event. A neutral point of view is established by bringing the camera level with the subject, neither looking up nor down on this event or person, and by using an appropriate lens for the size of the shot and required depth of field.

Framing, Continuity and Point of View (POV)

Where is the subject in the frame? Are they on the left, middle, or right? Sitting or standing? Are they looking toward the center or speaking off-camera? What is the reason for where they are in the frame? Why this composition? Does it make sense for continuity? What else will be seen in the frame? Will all of this coverage be able to be edited with continuity between shots? Continuity and location integrity are essential considerations for directors. Images need to connect in a cinematically logical way. For example, someone seen leaving the frame from the screen right should enter the next shot frame from the screen left. Entering from the screen right gives the impression that this person has turned around. If an interviewee is wearing a hat in one shot and no hat in the next shot, there is a break in continuity unless we see them remove the hat.

Shooting

Shooting a documentary film is different from shooting a theatrical movie. The "actors" in the documentary story are real people in real-life situations doing something being recorded. There are no sets, only locations not built to make films. However, in some nonfiction films and other cases, a set might be created to do an interview or facilitate some environment that isn't available. Shooting in someone's home or office requires several considerations. The footage must provide the look and feel of the location. Good exposures and places to set up the camera for the best composition of shots are also important. Most homes will have 15-amp or 20-amp circuit breakers that limit the number of watts (Approximately 1500 watts and 2000 watts, based on Ohms Law: Amps x Volts = Watts) that may be used on each line. Lighting opportunities may be limited. Offices may have higher amp lines, but office equipment on those lines might crash if a circuit is blown. Usually, a homeowner can identify the best place to plug in lights. Office buildings typically have an electrician or building supervisor who can help. (In many instances, offering this person a gratuity for assistance is not unusual. It should be in the budget.) If it's impossible to scout a location in advance, some extra time can be allowed to check things out on arrival. When interviewing someone in their home, look for where they will be comfortable, offering the best light and the least noise. Often all that can be done in a room is to bounce some light off the ceiling for fill light and bring up the overall lighting for good exposure.

Documentary film crews are small, mobile, and can work in tight spaces and environments where other events occur. Available light is often all that can be accommodated. However, when possible, it is desirable to enhance the available light. In exterior situations, "Flex fills" or other reflective implements or methods can be used to bounce fill light into shadows on faces or scenes. Documentary crews must work quietly and inconspicuously for many reasons, including not interfering with what is being documented. By working quietly and blending into the environment, the subjects can relax and be themselves. Have a second AD or PA quietly control bystanders in outdoor locations or at significant events to give the camera operator and director space to work. Locations should be checked in advance to see what is required. Location releases or permits may be necessary in some cases, such as public parks and city streets. Many cities do not require a permit for documentary crews if they are not using a tripod and no actors or on-camera talent are involved. Check with local governments.

Coverage

It is the director's responsibility to get adequate coverage of the subject. This includes shots that can be edited together seamlessly. Other footage may be used to demonstrate what the interviewee is talking about or show a reaction to what is being said, for example, someone listening. Additional coverage in the form of inserts and cutaways is also necessary. Planning is an excellent way to ensure that adequate coverage is obtained. The director can plan each shot, angle, and camera movement in a fiction production. Scenes and actors can be rehearsed to achieve maximum cinematic and dramatic potential. Documentaries require spontaneous coverage of action, events, and subjects. There is little time to set up and stage shots. Even if time permits, staging and rehearsing action (that involves the participants being documented) will create fiction instead of nonfiction. A documentary director must be able to visualize how a series of shots will be edited as they are being shot. The director must understand cinematic concepts and rules and apply them spontaneously as events unfold.

Shot Composition

The director asks for the type of shot they need and works with the director of photography and camera operator to compose each shot. For example, how much focus is required in front (near) and behind (far) the subject? Composing shots for a documentary film is important from many standpoints. Most of the same rules for theatrical films are also used for documentaries. The wider the lens, the more depth of field. The lower the millimeters, the wider angle of the lens. Based on a 35 mm format, a 24 mm lens has a wider angle and more depth of field than a 50 mm lens.

Depth of field is an area that is in focus, in front of (near) and behind (far), at the point where the lens is focused.

LENSES

Two types of lenses are used in film and digital video production: multi-focal length lenses (zoom lenses) and fixed focal length lenses (prime lenses). Documentary productions use zoom lenses for convenience and because many camcorders do not allow attached zoom lenses to be removed. Recent digital cine and Digital Single Lens Reflex (DSLR) cameras allow changing lenses.

Normal is relative to the format being used. Most 35 mm, full frame cameras use a 50 mm lens. Some CMOS DSLRs use higher millimeters to facilitate a 16 x 9 HD format. Professional camcorders use compensated 35 mm equivalents. A "normal" lens approximates what the human eye sees at any given distance based on the type of camera and format in use.

Wide Angle lenses show a wider field of view than a normal lens. An 18mm lens has more depth of field than a 50mm normal lens or a 100mm telephoto lens.

Telephoto lenses (long lenses) make distant images appear close by magnification. A focused telephoto lens has the least amount of depth of field. It optically compresses the image vertically, stacking up and flattening the image. When using a multi-focal lens, "zooming in" changes the focal length to the telephoto end of the lens. "Zooming out" is moving to the wide-angle end of the lens. A zoom-in to an object differs significantly from a dolly into the same subject. A zoom-in changes the focal length of the lens from wide to telephoto, thereby changing the size of the shot and compressing the image vertically. The depth of field also changes and becomes shallow. A dolly-in, moving the camera closer to the subject, maintains the same focal length, moving closer to the subject physically instead of optically. The two moves have different feels and are visually different. Choose a lens that best conveys the image in context with the story.

Standard Abbreviations for Shot Sizes

Extreme Close-up -- ECU

Close-up -- CU

Medium Close-Up -- MCU

Long Shot -- LS

Over-the-Shoulder -- OTS

Wide Shot -- WS

Full Shot -- FS

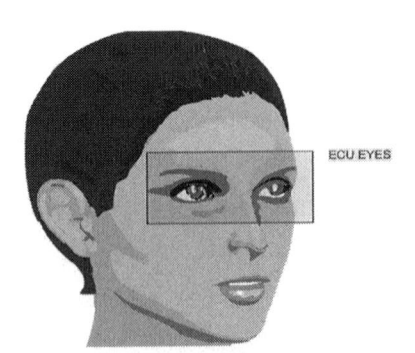

Tight CU Sends message: Look here!

THE DIRECTOR AND PRODUCTION CHAPTER 4

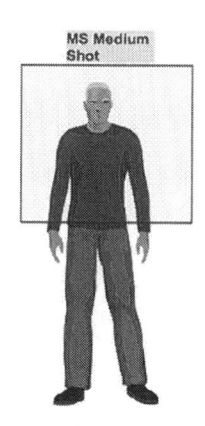

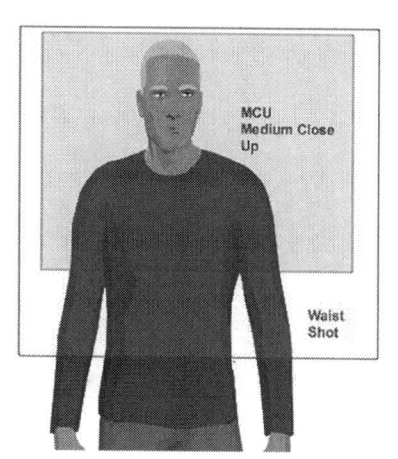

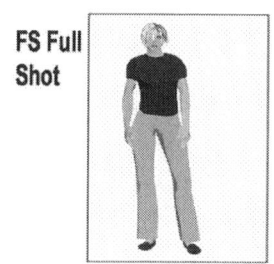

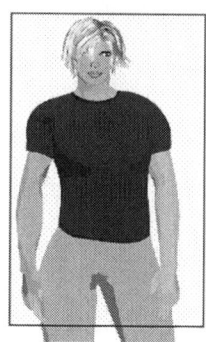

CU

LS

ECU
Tight CU
CU

MS Medium Shot

MCU Medium Close Up

Waist Shot

FS Full Shot

MFS Medium Full Shot

Avoid Shot! Awkward cut off around knee.

*Over the Shoulder CU and WS requires wide angle
lens to obtain background focus..*

Wide Shot (WS)

LS Long Shot

Shot Angles

When setting up a shot, the director considers the angle and the camera's placement. During an interview, the subject looks at the person conducting the interview. The camera captures that relationship. Is the interviewer standing? Is the interviewee sitting? Does this require the interviewee to look up at the interviewer? Framing and camera angles create a point of view and send a message to the audience. This idea applies to human subjects, inanimate objects, landscapes, machines, crowds, etc.

In an interview, a camera angle that looks down on a sitting subject conveys a condescending point of view. A low angle looking up at the interviewee may give a distorted or overbearing feel to the point of view.

If the interviewer and interviewee are both sitting or standing, a neutral point-of-view is to have the camera level with the subject and interviewer. If possible, avoid situations where the interviewer conducts the interview standing while the interviewee is sitting. Either have the interviewee stand or the interviewer sit down and bring the camera level with both parties.

Eye Lines in Interview Situations

There are two choices when it comes to interviewing a subject regarding where the interviewee's eye line may be directed. In most documentary situations, the interviewee should look at the interviewer, not the camera. Even though the interviewer and the questions may be cut out in editing, an interviewee who looks directly at the camera speaks directly to the audience "out there" somewhere. When the interviewee speaks to the interviewer, it is more intimate, and the viewer feels like they are at the location.

Television newscasters speak directly to the camera to

Camera is level with subject who looks at Director or Interviewer, not the camera. Composition keeps subject in TV safe area of the High Definition(HD) Frame..

establish a connection with the viewer. They report the news to the audience, so this simulated eye contact is necessary. This changes when there is an on-camera interview on the newscast. Eye lines are directed at the other person in the conversation, not the viewer. This creates a conversational atmosphere. Sometimes, where expert opinion or advice for the television audience is required, the interviewee may turn from the show anchor and talk to the camera addressing viewers directly

COMPOSITION

Documentaries and nonfiction visual presentations adhere to the exact compositional requirements of other visual mediums. Shots are composed within a rectangular frame. Movement occurs in this frame. In theatrical films, as well as television, there are technical advances that allow for more options when composing shots. For example, early video recording did not easily facilitate varying the depth of field in an image. Everything in the image was in focus. Today it is possible to create a shallow focus on a subject with the background out of focus (shallow depth of field) in digital video. Changing focus from the foreground to an object in the background (rack focus) or vice versa.

Composition within the frame adheres to the same photographic and artistic compositional guidelines that painters and photographers have used for centuries. Directors can study and be familiar with concepts like "vanishing perspective" and "negative space, among many other ideas about color, texture, composition, and movement. Understanding and use of these concepts can help tell the story.

The wine glass shape in between the two women is called "negative space." The subjects are the positive space. This negative shape has a form that confuses the viewer about what to look at in the frame.

Moving the subjects closer together helps eliminate the negative space.

Film Aspect Ratios

The aspect ratio is the relationship between the height and width of the frame, which is the actual shape of the frame. Not many documentaries are shot using film these days. The widescreen film aspect ratio is 1:85. This aspect ratio is shot using standard 35 mm film stock with a 1:33 aspect ratio frame. Later a mask is applied to the top and bottom of the frame converting the frame to make a 1:85 ratio.

Television Aspect Ratios

Standard Definition Television once had an aspect ratio of 4:3. Four units wide by three units high. Modern television aspect ratio conforms to a 16 x 9 aspect ratio. Shots must be composed to fit into this shape. However, not everything in the frame will be seen on every monitor. Action and graphics are composed to occur in an area called TV Safe. This is an area that will be seen on all televisions.

Lighting Choices Help Tell the Story

Documentary productions are always on the move. Shooting is in locations where the main light source is the "available light." Reflectors or Flex Fills, a light kit with several portable lights, a camera light, and LED lights, are usually part of a documentary production package. In addition, camera filters and various gels and diffusion are necessary tools..

Shooting Exteriors With Available Light

Exterior shooting is less problematic on an overcast day because the light is diffused and has less contrast. When shooting video, white balancing is necessary, as the color temperature will vary for each location. Be careful of a bright background behind the subject. If the auto iris function on the camera is used, it will calculate exposure for the brightest part of the environment, not necessarily the subject. Use a flex fill to bounce some light onto the subject, even though it may be subtle. On a heavily overcast day, reflect the fill light off the flex fill with a portable light instead of pointing the light directly at the subject for a softer look.

Try putting the subject in a shadow area in bright sunlight and always shoot with the sun behind the camera. A flex fill may be used in this instance as well. If you must shoot against the sun, use the flex fill to bounce as much light onto the subject as possible. Exposure should be set for the subject, exclusive of the background in this case. The background may become overexposed.

To shoot exterior interviews at night, find pools of light created by streetlights, windows, and other sources. Portable lamps can be mounted on the camera or set up to light the subject. Bounce the portable light off a flex fill or other reflectors for a softer feel rather than a harsher television news look. Always white balance for the available light. A flex fill can bounce the light from a well-lit window to fill in the opposite side of the interviewed person.

Lighting Interior Locations

Many subjects for documentary projects are shot under not ideal conditions, in offices, at events, in factories, on the street, and in dangerous or hostile environments. Lighting is essential in getting a properly exposed picture. Indoor lighting may vary, from daylight and tungsten in homes to daylight and fluorescent in office situations. There may be mixed lighting sources with varying color temperatures in the same room. A light kit with a few lights will help with supplemental lighting, but often it's about working with available light. Many offices have a person's desk located in front of a window. There are multiple possible lighting choices. If blinds or drapes are on the windows, see if they can be drawn and use lights for a simple key, fill, and backlight.

What if there is no way to block the light from the window? Consider shooting the interview using available light. Use the light coming from the window as a key light. For example, shooting the interview from an angle or the side of the desk might be possible. The light coming from the window is the key light, and a reflector is used to bounce in fill light. The subject faces the camera, and both are parallel to the window. Remember to white balance for daylight.

Consider lighting a subject with a key, fill, and backlight, whether available light, lighting instruments, reflectors, or a combination of sources. A key-to-fill ratio between two to one and four to one is ideal for most video interviews and other documentary situations. Appropriate, subjective lighting may be used to obtain a particular look or feel for an interview. However, most of the time, in documentary situations, the goal is to capture the texture of the environment. Therefore, reinforce the existing lighting so that a good exposure is obtained without adding another layer of interpretation.

Working with Fluorescent Lights

The biggest problem with fluorescent lights is that they have a high color temperature and may have a visible flicker. If possible, turn them off and light the area. In countries with fifty-cycle electrical currents, like Great Britain, a flicker might be seen in sync with the picture if you shoot at 25 or 24 fps. In the US, with sixty cycle electrical current, the problem may occur shooting video at 30 FPS.

Turning off the fluorescent lights may be impractical in many instances, so working with what's there is necessary. Camera filters can be used to change the color temperature. If using filmstock, sometimes daylight-balanced filmstock works better than a tungsten-balanced stock since the fluorescent color temperature is closer to daylight than tungsten. Offices are full of fluorescent lighting, which isn't as problematic for good digital camcorders as for film. White balance the camcorder under the fluorescent light, and the color balance should look natural. Any additional light used can be filtered to match the fluorescent

Working in Large Spaces

When it is impossible to light the entire space, one solution is to bounce light off the ceiling or walls to raise the overall light levels in a room with fluorescent lights. Use daylight balancing gels on your lights.

With video, "white-balancing," the camera is essential. The camera operator aims the camera at a white card and white balances the camera. When it is impossible to use a white card, the camera operator will look for something white in the scene to white balance the camera—even auto-white-balancing options on a camera need to see something white to use for balancing. The camera operator may zoom into someone wearing a white shirt or any white object in the shot

Covering Events, Meetings, Parades, Rallies, and Other Situations

Often, a director must cover various events used in the documentary as supplemental or "B" roll footage. The actual shots will not be scripted. This type of assignment may be given to a second unit director while the primary director is doing interviews or at another location. The second unit crew might have a camera operator and sound recordist work with the director. With such an assignment, one of the first things to do is to shoot establishing shots of the venue and any signs or banners identifying the event or venue. Shots of people arriving and or getting seated are also good to obtain. If there is a prominent speaker's platform, finding an unobstructed camera position is essential. Discuss options for recording the speakers with the sound recordist.

Events are not static situations. People may move around. The event has a beginning, middle, and end. Various things happen, and people react. Is this event central to the story, or is it just one of many similar events that might be included for a few seconds in the final documentary? Unless the assignment is to shoot the entire event for archival purposes, the director must determine what parts to cover so that an editor can cut a scene that, in a minute or less, gives the viewer a feel for that particular event.

The director is looking for some basic coverage and will choose what parts of the event to shoot. The first assistant director, script supervisor, or director can talk to the event organizers about the program and get a copy of the agenda, perhaps a copy of the speech, press release, and list of speakers if available. After filming some opening remarks, the crew is on standby to get additional footage of the main parts of the speech or the "best sound bites." The director listens to speakers and determines what to shoot. In all likelihood, whatever is shot will be used as needed. For example, a shot of someone holding a sign might be used to open the scene somewhere in the middle or at the end of the scene. Shots like this are part of getting "B" roll footage.

Suppose the main speaker for an event in an ample space is coming through the hall's main door with his entourage of security, politicians, and campaign workers. The camera crew tries to set up in a position to capture this action as the speaker makes their way to the stage. Maybe a sturdy table is obtained and used as a platform to give the camera operator some height to shoot from. The camera could then capture the entrance and stay with the speaker as they approached the stage. If no platform is available, the camera operator and assistant move backward in front of the speaker, recording them as they move toward the stage. They are working in the middle of the crowd, so the camera assistant is leading the camera operator. Following the speaker from behind to the stage is not the best shot. The back of the group's heads and bodies are not as interesting. Additional crew members can do crowd control around the camera. An experienced camera operator must walk backward and keep a handheld, well-framed shot. If available, a Steadicam can be used in situations like this.

It's a good idea to shoot footage of speakers being introduced. How long to continue with each speaker is the director's call. This is based on listening to the speakers and getting a sense of what they are talking about and where their speech is going. It is possible to start and stop shooting a speaker to pick up critical parts of the address. Usually, a speaker will end the talk with some conclusion which may be shot. If it is a short speech, it can all be recorded. When the audience applauds someone on the stage, the camera might swing around and film some applause shots. Afterward, the camera returns to the stage as the speaker continues. This type of shot has many uses, so the pans should be smooth. Complete coverage of this type of event includes several audience reaction shots. Get shots of people listening or not listening, laughing, holding signs, other people on the stage, camera crews, and long shots of the room and stage. These shots will allow the editor flexibility in the cutting room. In many documentary situations, there is only one camera to get all the coverage.

Camera Movement

The motion picture medium is built on two fundamental ideas. The first is that what is seen on the screen is moving and that the camera recording the movement can also be moved. In the early days of cinema, filmmakers didn't move the camera. They set up what is known as the "proscenium" shot. In this position, the camera is set up as if it had the best seat in the theater for viewing a stage play. It took a while before it was realized that the camera could be moved, thereby picking and choosing various points of view that would bring the audience into the story.

Today, documentary filmmakers use the lightness and portability of modern film and digital video cameras to take the audience where "no one has gone before." The camera moving as a pan from the speaker to the audience or the audience to the speaker can facilitate a transition between two shots. Moving the camera or changing the size of an image makes a statement. A move from a speaker to someone listening is an action and reaction. At times the whole pan may be used. At other times the pan might be cut, leaving two separate shots. At times, just before the shot becomes static, part of the pan might be used if cutting from another action shot. Cutting from one static image to another is okay, but there may be other alternatives if there is good coverage. Before starting a pan or tracking shot, think about where it will end. A tracking shot of someone walking leads the walker and either stops moving with the walker or stops, and the walker walks out of the picture. Leading leaves more space in front of the subject than behind in the frame. Experienced camera operators know to hold on to a shot for a beat or two before panning or cutting. The hold allows for room to cut in editing. Pans and tilts need to be at a steady pace that the viewer can read. Too fast or jerky moves bring attention to the camera.

CINEMATIC CONVENTIONS

There are many cinematic conventions that audiences have come to accept and expect. As was mentioned previously, regarding screen direction, if a subject leaves the screen frame on one side and enters the frame in the next shot from the same side, there is a feeling that the subject has turned around. If they enter from the other side of the screen, they are perceived to be continuing in the same direction. Directors need to visualize how scenes will be cut while shooting to allow for continuity and facilitate editing. Screen direction is a crucial element in maintaining continuity.

One of the oldest conventions regarding screen direction is that opposing forces or enemies come from opposite sides of the screen toward each other. Cars that will crash come from opposite directions. If we have two opposing groups in a documentary context, it might be natural to construct compositions that reinforce that opposition. Interviewees with opposing viewpoints might occupy different sides of the frame. In effect, they would be facing each other in their opposition.

Also important is maintaining a relationship between related elements in a scene. Suppose there is a crowd watching a football game in a stadium. Close-ups of spectators have a connection to the action on the field. This may require shooting from only one side of the stadium. Intercutting shots from the other side of the field have the spectators looking in the opposite direction from the action on the screen. It's called "crossing the line." This is an imaginary line that the camera should not cross to maintain the continuity of screen direction and eye lines. The move across the field can be shown on camera to change the perspective.

Eye lines are also important when covering a large group of people in a room or outdoor event. Once the space is established, the viewer is familiar with the room or outdoor space. For example, the stage has a place in the frame at a concert. The viewers feel they know where the stage is in the frame. Suppose someone points at the stage in an interview, but because of the way it is shot, they appear to point in the wrong direction. This can quickly happen based on where the interviewer stands and on what side of the camera. To prevent this type of "crossing the line" in these situations, the person conducting the interview must stay on one side of the camera in every shot. It can be either side but always the same side. In this case, the "line" is the camera.

Another example is covering a group sitting around a conference table with one camera. The individuals at the table speak to each other, and the conversations need coverage. Getting shots of two people who are on opposite sides of the table might appear to be "crossing the line." People on opposite sides of the table might appear to be looking the wrong way when speaking to someone across the table. The solution is to shoot the reverse angle of the other person over the same shoulder as was used for the first person. If person "B" was shot from over the right shoulder of person "A," then to get the reaction shot of person "A" shoot over person "Bs" right shoulder. All shots of everyone at the table must be over the opposite person's left shoulder exclusively or right shoulder exclusively. By keeping this uniform approach, everyone at the table will always look in the correct direction. All the eye lines will match.

More on Coverage

Another important coverage component is getting support footage or photographs based on what the interviewee is talking about. If someone is talking about a certain experience or environment, they can be asked if they have any photographs from that time. The camera operator can shoot these photographs while there on location. This is "B" roll that may be used in editing to show what the subject is referring to and/or to break up long sequences. The script supervisor or someone else can write down details about the photographs or other materials being recorded.

Coverage can include shots of where the interview is taking place or anything the interviewee mentions. A script supervisor who is there with the director listening to the interview makes notes about what is talked about and passes them along to the director. The camera operator is free to do some pickup shots based on something he or she has observed that might be useful.

Final Cut Pro on Laptop

Editing is a creative process involving the construction of a visual story or narrative. Editing is where the story is finally built and structured.

Desktop Editing

Chapter 5

The Director and Postproduction

The Director's involvement in postproduction for a documentary is often more extensive than in a fiction film project because the director may be deeply involved as a filmmaker, director, and producer.

A documentary director may have a deep commitment and involvement in a project. They may want to direct and edit. However, an experienced editor should do the editing. There are a few reasons for this idea. An editor provides a fresh approach and helps avoid the natural tendency toward unintentional, self-indulgent editing on the part of the director editing independently. The director and editor work as a team.

Postproduction for documentary films and videos follows much the same process as editing for fiction projects. The primary purpose is the editing and finishing of the film or video. One of the first things that get done while shooting and in postproduction for digital video formats is to back up all the video—at least two backups of all the original footage on separate drives. Save original camera flash drives if available. Next, capture the footage into whatever editing program is being used. Apple Final Cut, Adobe Premier Pro, and Avid offer "Studio" versions of their Software. Final Cut, Premiere Pro, and Avid include specialized applications for all advanced aspects of digital editing. Other programs like Adobe After Effects, Photoshop, and audio editing applications are also useful.

Editor and Editing

Editing is a creative process involving the construction of a visual story or narrative. Editing is where the story is finally built and structured. Editing is more than a mechanical process of splicing shots together. It involves the same abilities and talents a musician uses for translating a score into music on a musical instrument. This is more than reading notes. It is feeling the rhythm and pacing of each scene and segment and building the entire film into something more significant than the sum of its parts. It is knowing when, where, and how to make the next cut so that action flows and cuts are invisible. There is a creative collaboration between the editor and the director.

Reviewing Coverage

Review all the footage. Make written transcriptions of all the interviews. There are online voice recognition software and services available that can transcribe recorded interviews to word processing software. Having a transcription of the interviews is an asset for finding the most valuable parts of the interviews. Log all the Action and "B" roll footage so that it is easy to find. This work will help write the Editing Script (aka paper edit). On large projects, the editor may need assistant editors.

The director and the editor review the footage and transcriptions, looking for the best action, interviews, and "B" roll for each scene. They also review the original concept, treatment, and shooting script. After this process, an editing script or "paper edit" is written. The director may consult with a writer when creating the editing script. First-person interviews can be used to create a narrative. If voice-over narration is anticipated, narration for editing may be scripted, but the final narration is written once the film has taken shape.

Editing Script

Writing an editing script is an essential step in creating a story. It is an opportunity to review all the footage and to talk with consultants and knowledgeable people about ideas. It is a chance to find and explore the footage. Are there parallel themes that can be used? It is the time to develop the story, beginning, middle, and end, based on what has been shot.

A shooting or editing script for a documentary or nonfiction project looks much the same. They both use a multi-column format beginning with two columns, one for picture and one for audio. Additional columns may be added for storyboarding or other information. For example, a column for shot number and another for time is useful. If the editing script needs outside approval, frames from the footage can be included in one column.

The significant difference between a shooting script and an editing script is that the editing script is based on the footage shot and actual dialogue or interviews obtained. The shooting script is a starting point but may be modified based on new information or ideas. (See pages 138-141 for the editing script example).

Rough Cut

The film's first edit based on the editing script is called a rough cut. Once a rough cut is edited, it should be screened and reviewed to see how the cuts and pacing are working and how the story plays. The rough cut should be watched on a large screen monitor or projected on a screen. The rough cut is what the word "rough" implies. There may be missing shots, only the dialogue tracks, no effects, and partially still an assembly of scenes. It is a rough edit of the entire story, not just a few scenes. On longer films, a rough cut of specific segments may be screened.

Getting a natural feeling for the edit at this point is problematic on a small editing monitor. In addition, seeing the film on a large screen magnifies all the cuts. Audio heard over larger speakers helps to listen to things that might be missed on the smaller speakers. It is also a good idea to bring in consultants, trusted advisors, or someone who has yet to work on the film for a reaction at this time. This is not a screening for general viewers. You want informed persons who will be candid. You may judge their responses based on their expertise, either on the subject or as filmmakers. This is also an excellent time to think about music and effects for the film. The composer should be invited to the rough-cut screening if original music is required. Additional screenings as the edit proceeds are a good idea too.

Fine Cut

After screening the rough cut, it's time to start evolving a fine cut, creating effects and music tracks in addition to the two dialogue tracks already created. Audio is an integral part of editing and plays a significant role in telling the story. Audio for films and videos falls into three areas: dialogue, effects, and music. At the start of editing, begin with two dialogue tracks to edit dialogue as you go along inventively. Some editors might put all dialogue onto one track, "butt splicing" it together. Later, they break the audio up into multiple dialogue tracks. This is not very practical and sets up the possibility of mistakes and bad audio cuts. With digital editing software having multiple audio tracks available, splitting tracks from the start is a good idea and not challenging.

Audio Tracks

It is much better to start with two audio tracks for dialogue so that later, the process of equalizing, crossfading, or pulling up the sound for "J" cuts is facilitated. It is a problem getting to the point where you want to crossfade between tracks only to find that you don't have the additional frames available.

Multiple dialogue tracks are needed because each person's voice requires equalization, even if recorded in the same room. But especially when cutting between interviews at various locations. Ambient room tones differ depending on the time of day, the weather, and the number of people in a room. Listen carefully to all dialogue tracks for extraneous noise or comments off-camera.

Music

After working on dialogue, work on music tracks and effect tracks. There are situations when specific pacing of shots is necessary. Until the final music track is available, something with the same beat can be substituted to establish the editing rhythm.

Cutting dialogue or action to a musical scratch track may be desirable. Even when the final music is added to a fine cut, some tweaking may be needed to sync the piece with the editing. There must also be at least two music editing tracks to facilitate cross fading the music or fading music out under some action in the next scene. Documentaries may make use of "source" music. This is music that was recorded on location while filming. It becomes part of the documentary story. Composers like a fine-cut copy of the documentary to compose their score. Hopefully, once the music is recorded, there will be no changes to the scenes where the music is needed.

Effects

Documentary films require effects edited into the story. Multiple tracks are usually needed for effects. Effects tracks may include room tone and location ambiance. Location ambient sound is needed to bring a cutaway shot or still photograph to life. Effects, like a bird chirping, bring a photographic landscape to life. All the "B" roll footage should have been shot with audio. If not, another ambient sound can be used. The shot's audio is included with the picture when edited into the film. It may be a subtle presence under voice or with music, but an actuality dimension is lost without it.

Keep your dialogue, music, and effect tracks in separate groups that can be pre-mixed into the three categories: dialogue, music, and effects. When editing is complete, the dialogue, music, and effects will be mixed into a final three-track recording as a final mix. There are several reasons for this process. Keeping dialogue, music, and effects separate allows an editor to return to any of the three areas without disturbing the other tracks. This helps the mixing engineer in setting levels during the final mix. It is also practical if dialogue ever needs to be dubbed. As the fine cut of the documentary evolves, scenes are tightened up, and changes are made to eliminate those shots that may not seem to work. Using a digital editing program facilitates re-reverting to a previously saved version, so do not be afraid to experiment. Documentary and fiction have similar priorities, including pacing, timing, and continuity. Editing can make or break a production. Here are some basic guidelines to think about while editing. Directors understand editing.

Basic Post Production and Editing Guidelines

Edit for content. Do not stretch scenes. The time to cut from a shot is when the action ends, and the new action begins in the following image. When a cut is made to a new image, something should happen. Once the current shot's purpose is accomplished, it's time to move on to the next shot.

Motion pictures rely on motion, action, and reaction. Action motivates cutting. Each cut must be motivated. For example, someone throws a ball in the first shot, and someone catches it in the following image. There are many ways to edit this action, but in the end, it is an action followed by a reaction. Eye movements may motivate a cut to the next shot. Other more subtle movements in the shot can also help. A camera movement in the image can motivate the cut and carry the viewer into the next shot.

Interview dialogue or reactions motivate a cut to the next shot. For example, an interviewee finishes talking, and the voice-over of someone else is heard (still in the first shot) before cutting to that second person. This type of transition motivates the cut and helps story pacing. A variation allows the dialogue in one shot to carry over to the next shot as a voice-over while the next person reacts to what the first person is talking about.

Avoid long sequences of talking heads. Even with various shots covering an interview, it gets difficult for an audience to stay awake while listening. The action keeps the pace moving. If coverage is adequate, the editor should have some cutaways and footage to break up the interview. For example, if someone is talking about their hometown, pictures of the town or this person growing up there can be used with their voiceover.

Continuity between shots and scenes is essential. For example, interviews with the same person on different days may result in that person being dressed differently. Cutting the two interviews together may be confusing to the viewer. However, if there are some other shots or scenes in between, it will soften the difference.

Parallel themes create a story that goes beyond a basic linear progression. For example, suppose four people are being interviewed about their lives. Instead of doing one person's life, then the next, the interviews can be edited on various themes, like growing up, work, religion, and other topics. Each person's experience is contrasted in some way with the other interviewees.

In Chapter Four, three types of scenes are mentioned. Action with No Dialogue, Dialogue with No Action, and Action and Dialogue. Each of these types of scenes requires certain kinds of editing. Each of these types of scenes must be shot to facilitate their editing.

Screen direction is a priority when editing an action scene, for example, a scene about a five-kilometer footrace. The concept for the scene is to edit the event from start to finish with some color before and after the race. But the central part of the clip is the race itself. If the director has done their job covering the event, there will be continuity of screen direction for the race over the length of the course. Fundamental conventions like "crossing the line" become important as the editor puts together a compilation of runners starting the race, running the course, and coming across the finish line. How the runners are shot over the race route must connect in a way that preserves screen direction, continuity, and spectator reaction, so the edited version feels right on the screen. That great CU of a runner's feet hitting the ground must show the feet going in the same direction as the runner!

Scenes with no action and only dialogue require coverage that includes a variety of shots, cutaways, inserts, and general "B" roll. Interviews need more than one locked-off shot. Vary the size of the image during the interview.

Action and dialogue or Action only scenes help the pace and editing of the film. For example, that five-kilometer race becomes dynamic with interviews and shots of runners before and after the race can be cut to when we see the same runners during the race. Hearing a few lines of an interview as they are running in the race helps tell the story. Shots of spectators, individual runners, and flashbacks from interviews or warming up add depth and layers to the story.

Transcripts

A transcript of all the dialogue in the film needs to be made when a fine cut of the documentary is finished. This is especially important if subtitles will be used for other languages.

Test Screenings

Screen the fine cut to associates and friends to get reactions. Bring in a cross-section of people whose responses to certain things might be predictable. For example, another editor might pick up editorial problems. An expert in a particular area that the documentary deals with is thinking about the subject matter more than how the film is cut. Test screenings are not meant for critical reviews of the story or subject but for getting audience reactions and technical feedback. Know who the audience is for each screening and consider comments accordingly.

Even when a director works with an editor, there is a tendency for self-indulgence, in that both individuals become committed to ideas that might have problems. Bring in the DP to give feedback on color correction, the audio engineer to listen to the sound, and the script supervisor who may pick up something that has been missed or may remember an alternative shot that solves an editorial problem. Bring in consultants who can check for factual or historical mistakes.

Final Fine Cut

After initial in-house screenings, some tweaking of the film is routine. The fine cut is usually test screened without a final sound mix. There are three sets of audio tracks—Dialogue, Music, and Effects. The editor prepares separate tracks for each group. There may be two or more dialogue tracks. Also, multiple music and effects tracks. It is easy to keep these groups of tracks separate using editing software. For example, dialogue tracks first, then effects, and then music.

In a professional situation, a recording engineer mixes the tracks during a final mix session. The engineer has the experience, equipment, and software to balance all elements and tracks perfectly. For example, the music must be balanced, and levels set to not interfere with dialogue or voice-over. Effects or presence tracks are kept at appropriate levels for the action. Cross dissolves need to be created between scenes. Many issues with audio tracks can be corrected with sophisticated filters and software during the mix.

Audio Mix

An editor can do much with high-end audio editing software to create a final mix if professional mixing services are unavailable or the project only requires a simple audio mix. An editor may do a preliminary mix before a screening or professional mix session. This process begins with premixing each of the three elements (Dialogue, Music, and Effects) to set audio levels in these areas. Special attention is given to balancing and equalizing dialogue tracks. Also, music levels must not compete with the dialogue. Musical transitions can help soften cuts and provide continuity. Music crossfading between scenes transitions the viewer into the next scene. Action is always shot with an audio presence which must be equalized from scene to scene. It may only be a subtle presence, but it should be there. For example, during an interview, someone refers to the high traffic in the city. There is a cut to traffic with their voiceover. That shot of the traffic is incomplete without the presence of subtle traffic sounds. During a mix, all tracks are equalized and made to fit naturally. Hopefully, all is perfect after the final mix and a final test screening. Everyone has done their job, and the documentary is ready for theatrical release or prime time.

Trailer

Did anyone cut a trailer? A trailer for a documentary film shares much in common with a trailer for a fiction film. Both need to introduce and sell the movie to a prospective audience. A script must be written, and editing must be approached like the original film is handled. The producer or the distribution company may have some good ideas on what will sell the film. They can come in early to start working on developing ideas for the trailer. A trailer may be cut before or while the film is edited to promote the documentary online or in other venues. A trailer may be necessary to get entry into festivals. Review the original concept and treatment to help find critical ideas. There can be several trailers, each for a different venue.

Production Stills and Video

Another asset that will be needed is those production stills and behind-the-scenes videos that were shot while the documentary was being made. A short interview with the director/filmmaker about the film and its purpose: these can be used to promote the documentary before and after it is released.

Preview Screenings

Preview screenings and getting exposure to the documentary in film festivals are essential. Planning for these things can be done after the documentary is edited. Articles can be written about the story, and a preview screening date can be scheduled.

"I'm a filmmaker. I'm an artist. I've chosen to work in history the way someone might choose to work in still-life or landscapes."

-- Ken Burns

"People tend to forget that the word "history" contains the word "story."

-- Ken Burns

"Democracy is not a spectator sport, it's a participatory event. If we don't participate in it, it ceases to be a Democracy."

-- Michael Moore

"I believe that when you provide information to people, they become less fearful and they will engage more in their democracy if they are empowered with information."

-- Michael Moore

On Line Resources

Documentary Reviews

http://www.jrmartinmedia.com/documentary-film-reviews/

http://www.jrmartinmedia.com/category/documentary-reviews-2/

http://www.jrmartinmedia.com/

Bibliography

Alten, Stanley R. Audio In Media. Belmont, CA: Wadsworth Publishing 1986 Print

Barnouw, Erik. Documentary a history of the nonfiction film. New York: Oxford UP, 1993. Print

Carlson, Verne. Professional lighting handbook. Boston: Focal, 1985. Print.

Crowell, Thomas A. The Pocket Lawyer For Filmmakers. Boston: Focal Press 2007 Print

Grant, Barry K. and Sloniowski, Jeannette, Documenting the Documentary Close Readings of Documentary Film and Video. Detroit: Wayne State UP, 1998. Print.

Edmonds, Robert. Anthropology On Film. Dayton: Pflaum, 1974.

Family of Man the 30th anniversary edition of the classic book of photography. New York, N.Y: Museum, Distributed by Simon & Schuster, 1983. Print

Frankfurt, Harry G. On Truth. New York: Alfred A. Knopf, 2006. Print.

Garrand, Timothy Paul. Writing for multimedia entertainment, education, training, advertising, and the World Wide Web. Boston: Focal, 1997. Print.

Hampe, Barry. Making Documentary Films and Videos A Practical Guide to Planning, Filming, and Editing Documentaries. New York: Holt Paperbacks, 2007. Print.

Hardy, Forsyth. John Grierson. London and Boston: Faber and Faber, 1979. Print.

Holt, Jason. The Daily Show and Philosophy (The Blackwell Philosophy and Pop Culture Series). Grand Rapids: Blackwell, 2007. Print.

Houghton, Buck. What a producer does the art of moviemaking (not the business). Los Angeles: Silman-James, Distributed by Samuel French Trade, 1991. Print.

Jacobs, Lewis. The Documentary Tradition. Second ed. New York: W.W. Norton and Company, 1979. Print.

Katz, Steven D. Film Directing Shot by Shot, Visualizing from Concept to Screen, Michael Wiese Productions, 1991 Print

Konigsberg, Ira. The Complete Film Dictionary. New York: Meridian, 1987. Print.

Lumet, Sidney. Making movies. New York: Vintage, 1996. Print.

Martin, Clifford, Microphones how they work & how to use them. Blue Ridge Summit, Pa: G/L Tab, 1977. Print.

Martin, James R. Actuality Interviewing and Listening, How to Conduct Successful Interviews, Real Deal Press/J R Martin Media, Orlando, Florida 2018, 2023. Print and Digital

Martin James R. Create Documentary Films, Videos and Multimedia, Third Edition, Real Deal Press/J R Martin Media Inc, 2014, Print and Digital

Martin James R, Listen Learn Share, Real Deal Press/J R Martin Media Inc 2018, Print and Digital

Murch, Walter. In The Blink of an Eye. Second Edition. A Perspective on Film Editing. Sillman-James Press. 2001. Print

Wiese, Michael. Film & video budgets. Studio City, CA: M. Wiese Productions, 1995.

Index

A

Aaron, 61
Abel, 88
abstract, 51, 58, 161
abstraction, 117
abuse, 101
academic, 133, 143
academically, 97
academy, 22–23, 32, 40, 46, 58, 75, 80, 82,
  87–88, 98, 101, 110
accused, 55
acoustics, 149
act, 51–53, 63–64, 79, 86, 91–93, 104, 114
action, 19, 27–28, 33–34, 45, 47, 49, 51–53,
  61, 63, 72, 79, 88, 95, 98, 104, 107–108,
  111, 115–116, 119, 123, 127–128, 132,
  137–138, 145, 154, 161–163, 166, 174,
  178–182, 186–187, 189–193, 195
activist, 23, 59, 84
actors, 19, 38–39, 119–120, 136, 164–166
Actualities, 122
Adam, 51
adding, 176
addition, 34, 55, 67–68, 89, 112, 116, 133,
  174, 188

administration, 49, 111
adult, 94, 97, 104, 113
advertising, 60, 62–63
advocacy, 42–43, 75–76, 80, 82, 88, 94,
  99–100, 103, 107, 109, 121, 128–129
advocate, 39, 42, 87, 102, 121
advocating, 84, 121
Aeronautics, 111
Afghanistan, 36, 40–41
African, 73, 75
African Americans, 85
age, 22, 63–65, 88, 102–103, 113, 131
agency, 60, 96, 118, 133
agenda, 20, 88, 121, 131, 178
agreement, 145–146
Agreements, 152
Agriculture, 49
Akira, 43
Al, 75, 109, 111
Alabama, 84–85
Alain, 50
Albert, 69
album, 34, 110
Aldus, 106
Alex, 51
allies, 50, 92
amateur, 97
America, 32–33, 73–74, 84, 129
American, 23, 32, 42, 57, 62, 72–75, 84–85,
  91–94, 105, 109, 111, 113, 122
Amherst, 22

Amish, 103–104
amp, 164
analog, 146, 159–161
angle, 54, 67, 137–138, 158, 163, 166–167,
   170–171, 176, 182
animal, 23, 38, 76–78, 94
animated, 19, 32, 150, 163
animation, 19, 31–32, 119, 148
antagonist, 52–53, 132
anthropological, 60, 96, 104
Anthropologist, 56
Anthropologists, 55
anthropology, 54–55, 71, 104
Apple, 186
applications, 143, 186
Archaeology, 71
archival, 19, 22, 26, 34–35, 43, 51, 57,
   60–61, 63, 65–66, 68–69, 72, 76, 79, 83,
   85–89, 92, 100–101, 105, 107–108,
   110–111, 136, 143, 147, 178
armies, 122
arms, 163
Armstrong, 112
Aronson, 95
arrest, 83
art, 19, 22, 30–31, 39, 54–55, 58–60, 62–64,
   71, 75, 79, 81, 102, 110, 124, 151
article, 33, 97, 129, 142
Articles, 196
artifacts, 35, 50, 57

artificial, 156
Artinian, 95
artist, 31, 58–65, 73, 124
artistic, 58, 75, 123, 173
artistically, 59
arts, 22, 60
artwork, 31
assassination, 20, 88, 121
astronauts, 112
Athens, 52, 118
athletes, 52–53
atmosphere, 86, 172
atrocities, 85
attach, 124
attached, 58, 149, 167
attachment, 79
attack, 20, 83–84, 101, 107, 121
Attacking, 121
attackumentary, 121
audience, 43, 51, 53, 73, 109, 111, 114–116,
   124, 127–128, 132, 156, 159, 171–172,
   180–181, 192, 194–195
Audiences, 161
audio, 30–33, 38–39, 58, 74, 89, 92, 115,
   122, 134, 136, 138, 140–141, 147,
   157–158, 162, 186–190, 194–195
Auguste, 53
auteur, 25, 34
authentic, 120
authenticity, 29
author, 32, 71, 90, 105, 108

authority, 108
autobiographical, 31, 104
AV, 141
availability, 56, 94, 149
average, 94
Avid, 186
award, 22–23, 32, 40, 46, 53, 72, 75, 80, 82, 87–88, 90, 98, 101, 154
Awards, 110

B

backdrop, 73
background, 21, 60, 89, 110, 170, 173–175
backlight, 176
Baez, 84–85
Bagram, 41
Baichwal, 115
balance, 53, 175–177, 194
balanced, 29, 149, 177, 194
balancing, 174, 177, 195
Ballerina, 113
ballet, 113
band, 63, 66–67, 70, 162
Bangladesh, 116
banjo, 100
Bank, 46
Banksy, 59–60
banned, 93
Bansky, 59–60
Baptist, 84
baptized, 103–104
Barbara, 82
Barks, 105

barn, 141
barriers, 46–47
Barry, 61
Baseball, 73–74
basis, 29, 123, 132, 134–135
Battalion, 41
battery, 36, 41, 149
battlefield, 50
BBC, 22, 111
BCE, 102
beach, 116
bear, 37
beat, 190
beaten, 70
beautiful, 60–61, 74, 110
behavior, 53, 55
Beijing, 38, 58
Bengal, 80
Berkeley, 23
Berlin, 58
Bernie, 108
Bertha, 90
Bess, 113
Betrayal, 101
Bette, 111
BFA, 24, 38
biases, 46
Bible, 69
bicycle, 104
bigotry, 86–87
billboard, 62
biochemist, 94
biographical, 35
biography, 24, 34, 65, 75
bird, 56, 190

Birmingham, 84–86
black, 41, 50–51, 58, 72–73, 75–76, 85–86, 117
Blackfish, 76
blind, 50, 85, 176
blog, 33
blue, 112, 119
Blush, 110
Bob, 24, 66
Bobby, 67
bomb, 84
bombed, 85
bombing, 85
bookstore, 39
Boston, 111
Bowie, 110
Bowling, 23
Boxer, 63–65
boxing, 64
Brannaman, 107
breakdown, 145–146
Brian, 112
bride, 57
bridge, 22, 148
Bridgewater, 93
Briski, 80–82
Britain, 80, 93, 176
broadcast, 28, 65, 90, 117, 131
Brooklyn, 22
Brookside, 83
brothels, 80–82
brother, 30, 38, 69, 92, 96
Bruce, 104, 110–111
buck, 107
Buddhist, 45
Buddy, 22

budget, 26, 94, 134–135, 144, 147, 150, 150, 152–153, 164
budgeting, 141, 151
Budgets, 155
Bugliosi, 108
build, 61, 98, 112, 128, 133
bullets, 40
Bullie, 65
Burnet, 46
Burtynsky, 115–117

C

cable, 111, 117
Cabrini, 90–91
Calcutta, 80–81
Caldwell, 94
California, 24, 69, 89, 91, 98
cam, 34
camcorder, 59, 167, 177
camera, 19, 22, 25–26, 28–29, 36, 39, 41, 43, 46–47, 54, 56–57, 65, 67, 70, 72, 81–82, 88–89, 93, 98, 100, 108, 116, 123, 135–137, 145–149, 151, 153, 156–159, 162–167, 171–172, 174–180, 182–183, 186, 189, 191
cameraman, 93
cameraperson, 54, 56, 148
Cameras, 36, 41, 46–48
campaign, 62, 179
Campbell, 61, 94–95
camps, 50–51, 77, 83
Canada, 32, 52, 93, 102

Canadian, 52
cancer, 94–95
candid, 59, 117, 188
candidates, 131
candle, 63
canine, 96
Canon, 76
canvas, 64
capable, 98
capital, 48, 80
Capitalism, 43
captain, 155
captions, 64
capture, 38, 53, 56, 76, 112, 171, 176, 179, 186
captured, 50, 70, 76
capturing, 28
car, 70, 98
carcinogenic, 99
card, 177
care, 42, 77, 93–94, 98
career, 21, 23–24, 30, 66, 89, 96, 113
Carl, 30
Carol, 85
Caroll, 50
Cars, 181
cartridges, 36, 41
carved, 102–103
cash, 151
cashed, 87
cast, 20, 33, 65
casting, 58
cataloged, 71, 95
catalyst, 84
catastrophe, 87

catastrophic, 70
categorized, 119
categorizes, 58, 78
cave, 37–38, 102
CBS, 28, 117–118
ceiling, 165, 177
celebrate, 63, 110
celebration, 66
celebrities, 33
cell, 47, 56, 93, 140–141
celluloid, 160
censorship, 28
center, 84, 108, 112, 163
centered, 68, 102, 123
central, 105, 178
Century, 32
certain, 26–27, 33, 43–45, 54–57, 59, 76–77,
85, 87, 96, 104, 118, 120, 130–131,
135–137, 141, 144, 149, 155–156, 176,
183, 188–189, 192–194
certainly, 32, 42, 84, 106
champion, 82
championship, 98
changing, 56, 104, 167, 180
Channel, 75, 111, 117
Charles, 87, 108, 111
Charlotte, 69
Chauvet, 37
Chicago, 71, 90
Children, 130
Chin, 23
China, 32, 38, 58, 91–92, 95, 116–117

Chinese, 91–93, 95, 115–116
CHOICES, 174
Choir, 123
choral, 123
Chris, 61, 96, 115
Christian, 86
Christianity, 102
Chronicling, 115
chronological, 90
cine, 167
cinema, 18, 29, 34, 41, 59, 69, 93, 104, 115,
161, 163, 180
cinéma, 18, 29, 34, 41, 59, 84, 100, 115
cinematic, 28, 32, 50, 61, 114, 117, 123, 159, 166, 181
cinematically, 164
cinematographer, 22, 26, 43, 114, 146
cinematography, 22, 43, 65, 67, 81, 87, 107, 110, 114, 116
Circle, 33
circuit, 164
circumstance, 21, 33, 72, 134, 137, 141, 156
civilization, 74–75, 93, 106
Clan, 57
Clapton, 66
classmate, 22
Claudia, 110
Clayton, 110
clear, 23, 51–52, 63–64, 70, 76, 84, 86, 92,
94, 100, 117, 149, 158
Clervaux, 30

Cleveland, 94
clothing, 59
Clow, 62
CMOS, 167
CNN, 117
coach, 52, 97, 120
coal, 80, 82–83, 116
cochlear, 96
Cocker, 111
codirect, 57
Coleman, 105
Colin, 94
Collaborating, 56
collaboration, 43, 134, 186
collaborative, 56
college, 22, 71
Collins, 83, 85
color, 50–51, 117, 148, 159, 173–177, 192,
194
Columbia, 71
Columbine, 23
combat, 40–42
comedies, 20, 121
comfortable, 107, 165
coming, 45, 65, 70, 86, 91, 103, 129, 131,
157, 162, 175–176, 179, 193
command, 112
commanders, 102
commendable, 56
comment, 30, 64–65, 120, 189, 191, 194
commentary, 58, 62, 118, 124
commercial, 60, 118, 134, 139, 143
commercialization, 60

commitment, 25, 27, 185
committed, 85–86, 194
common, 27, 60, 195
communicate, 45, 51, 62, 78–79, 157–158
communicating, 147
communication, 147
community, 71, 73, 95, 97, 104
competition, 97, 113–114
competitive, 24, 52
compose, 166
composed, 58, 115, 122, 172, 174
composer, 188
composing, 166, 173
composition, 26, 74, 117, 148–149, 159, 163–164, 166, 172–173, 181
compound, 40
compressing, 167
concept, 25, 28, 44, 49, 90, 111, 132–134, 142–143, 150, 152, 166, 173, 187, 192, 196
Conceptualize, 133
concert, 53, 57, 65–71, 109, 182
conducts, 171
conference, 86, 182
conflict, 51, 78, 96–98, 100, 111, 114, 127–128, 132
conform, 92, 174
confrontation, 53
confronting, 84
confuse, 162, 173

Congo, 77
congressional, 49, 101
connect, 78, 93, 107, 164, 193
connected, 28, 42, 64, 102
connection, 18, 94, 172, 181
conscious, 105
consciousness, 45
conspiracy, 20, 121, 131
Constitution, 74, 87
constitutional, 84
construct, 22, 35, 50, 53, 62, 130, 156, 158, 181
constructed, 157
constructing, 34
construction, 22, 117, 149, 184, 186
consult, 26, 133, 187
consultants, 54, 132, 187–188, 194
contemporary, 28, 42, 60, 74, 105
content, 19, 31, 61, 78, 191
context, 27, 33, 39, 50, 58, 62, 72, 74, 78, 88, 122, 128, 154–155, 161, 163, 168, 181
Continental, 91
continents, 112
continuity, 137, 158, 162–164, 181–182, 191–193, 195
contract, 83
controversial, 43, 87, 89, 108, 117, 131
conversation, 32–33, 77, 88–89,

128–129, 138, 182
conversational, 172
copyright, 141–142
copyrighted, 142–143
Cornell, 94
corporate, 19, 26, 38, 104, 108, 113, 118, 122, 139, 147
corporation, 28, 118, 131
council, 71, 90, 142
country, 30, 47, 52, 73, 92–94, 99, 107, 112, 176
county, 82–84, 95
Courtney, 97
Cousteau, 23
Cove, 76
cover, 57, 67–68, 73, 102, 105, 114, 122, 132, 136, 141, 146, 157, 162, 178
coverage, 19, 28, 54, 56, 76, 79, 98, 100, 114–115, 131–132, 134–138, 145–146, 154–158, 162–163, 165–166, 178, 180, 182–183, 186, 192–193
covered, 29, 63, 95, 108, 131, 145, 147–148, 156, 163
covering, 67, 72, 156, 178, 182, 192
covey, 117
Cowperthwaite, 76
cramped, 82

creative, 62–63, 82, 90–91, 128, 184, 186
crew, 25–27, 55–56, 67, 83–84, 105, 135, 144–148, 151–153, 155–156, 158, 165, 178–180
crime, 101, 119
criminals, 81
Criminology, 71
Crips, 23
crisis, 87, 89, 98
criteria, 17, 30, 42, 84
critical, 17, 45, 83, 142, 194
criticism, 55
critics, 73
Cronkite, 86
crops, 102
crossover, 24
Crowell, 143
Cuban, 89
cultural, 32, 35, 46, 55, 90, 96, 98, 121
culturally, 72
culture, 47, 54–57, 60, 72–73, 79, 96, 102–103, 106, 109
curiosity, 130
current, 69, 71, 92, 98–99, 106, 129, 133, 176–177, 191
cut, 51, 59, 85, 135, 137, 150, 154, 162, 166, 171, 178, 180–181, 186, 188–196
Cutie, 63–65
cutting, 66, 154, 161, 180, 189–192

Cvetko, 87
Cynthia, 85

D
damage, 146
Damon, 87
Dan, 62, 78, 97
Dana, 51
dance, 113–115
dancer, 113–115
Dani, 56
Dark, 82
darkness, 159
Darlene, 110
Darwin, 106
David, 22–23, 28, 56, 62, 67, 69, 79, 105, 110, 117
Davidi, 46–47
Davis, 68, 75, 86
daylight, 175–177
deaf, 50, 95–96
deafness, 95
deconstruct, 108
default, 29, 53
defense, 89, 94, 102, 142
Democracy, 108
demographics, 128
Demography, 71
Denice, 85
depression, 43
depth, 35, 92, 95, 108, 110, 157, 163, 166–167, 173
depth of field, 163
design, 22, 27, 85, 87, 100, 108

Desmond, 105
Detective, 104
device, 63, 96, 117, 148, 159–160
devil, 70, 102–104
DGA, 25
diabetes, 94
dialog, 68, 89, 112, 115, 162–163, 187–195
dialogue, 26, 147–148, 160
diet, 93, 95, 123
diffused, 174
diffusion, 174
digital, 29, 114, 146, 157, 159–161, 166–167, 173, 177, 180, 186, 189, 191
digitally, 160
dime, 127
dimension, 68, 113, 115, 190
dimensional, 31
diorama, 31
direct, 18, 22, 24–25, 29, 34, 41, 59, 69, 92–93, 104, 115, 143–144, 161, 163
directed, 19, 43, 49, 51, 59, 62, 64, 66, 68, 71–72, 75–76, 78–79, 82, 85, 87, 91, 93–95, 103–105, 107–108, 110–111, 113, 115, 119, 171–172
directing, 17–18, 21, 24, 27, 44, 48, 60, 159
direction, 24, 158, 162, 181–183, 192–193
directly, 48, 89, 149, 158, 171–

172, 175
director, 18–19, 21–28, 33, 38, 45–47, 54,
56, 62–63, 67, 80, 88, 98–99, 104–105,
108, 114, 127, 133–135, 137, 143–159,
162, 164–166, 168, 171–172, 178–179,
183, 185–187, 192, 194, 196
Directors, 53–54, 97, 144, 173, 181
disabilities, 52
discrimination, 91
discuss, 20, 44, 87, 121, 133, 135, 137, 145,
156, 178
discussed, 88, 91, 129, 152
disease, 93–95
distributed, 28, 117–118
distribution, 49, 150–152, 196
DIY, 60
DJ, 63
DNA, 78
Doc, 63
docudrama, 118–119, 151
document, 18, 32, 34–35, 38, 47, 57, 59, 69,
72, 81–82, 87, 90
documentaries, 19–20, 30–33, 38–39, 49, 54,
60, 71–72, 88, 93, 96–97, 108–109, 120,
123, 130–131, 166, 172, 190
documentary, 16–35, 37–124, 127–139,
141–148, 150–151, 154–159, 161,
164–167, 171, 174–176, 178, 180–181,
185, 187, 190–191, 193–196
documentation, 30, 32, 34, 54, 69, 72, 92, 120
documented, 37, 56, 61, 65, 90, 95, 120, 129,
132, 139, 164–165
Documents, 50
Dogtown, 23
dolly, 151–152, 159, 167
dolphins, 76
domain, 142
domestic, 64, 131
domesticated, 78
DP, 25–26, 144, 146–149, 155–158, 194
Draft, 141
drama, 41, 51, 75, 84, 98, 114, 120
dramatic, 51–53, 66, 89, 109, 111–112, 114,
119–120, 124, 166
dramatically, 89
dramatized, 136
drawing, 34, 38, 40, 64–65
DRAWINgS, 31
drawn, 52, 84, 114, 176
Dreams, 37, 79
Drifters, 80
drives, 161, 186
drone, 57, 157
drug, 81, 93–94
DSLR, 76, 167

Dualism, 106
dualist, 106
dubbed, 190
Duke, 83
dusty, 82
duty, 80, 147, 151–152

DVD, 74
Dylan, 24, 66
dynamic, 193
dysfunctional, 97
Dziga, 28

E

earth, 37, 102–103, 112
East, 80
Eastern, 77
ecological, 80, 129
economics, 54, 71
ECU, 168
Edge, 68
edit, 25, 27, 46, 137, 154, 162, 186–189, 191–192
edited, 20, 32–34, 38, 54, 57, 60–61, 68–69, 76, 84–85, 90, 92, 96, 104–105, 107–108, 111, 121, 135, 137, 150, 163, 165–166, 188, 190, 192–193, 196
editing, 18, 25–26, 28–29, 39, 43, 50–51, 53, 57, 61, 63, 65, 69–70, 74, 82, 92, 98, 100, 104, 110, 116, 120, 135–136, 138–139, 141, 146, 158–159, 161, 171, 181, 183–192, 194–196
edition, 30
editor, 23, 25–26, 47, 88, 115, 150–151, 154, 158, 162, 178, 180, 185–187, 189–190, 192–195
editorial, 194
editorially, 89
educate, 48
education, 19, 31, 90–91
educational, 26, 31, 39, 78, 88, 90–92, 96, 103–104, 111, 119–120, 122, 128, 139, 142–144, 147, 151
Edward, 28, 30–31, 115, 117
Edwin, 65
effect, 32–33, 43–44, 72, 86, 88, 92, 98, 115, 148–149, 188–190, 194
effective, 87
effects, 186, 190, 194
effort, 58, 60, 103, 119, 151
ego, 128
Eisler, 50
Elaine, 22
election, 109
electric, 68, 98
electrical, 176
electrician, 164
electronic, 96, 159–160
electronically, 159–160
elusive, 47

Emad, 46–47
embedded, 40, 42, 75, 81
embellished, 37
emerged, 28
Emmy, 72, 90
Emmylou, 66
emotion, 68, 114, 128, 168
emotional, 43, 79, 160, 163
emotionally, 51
empathetic, 84, 107
empathy, 52
emphasis, 150
emphasize, 160
emphasizing, 58
employ, 20, 38–39, 129, 136
employed, 28, 38–39, 51, 147, 150
employing, 159
Endowment, 71
ENG, 149, 159
engineer, 190, 194
engines, 129
English, 103
enhance, 68, 148
environment, 19, 31, 41, 47, 51, 68, 73,
75–76, 79, 81–82, 98–99, 113–114, 117,
139, 148, 156–157, 164–165, 175–176, 183
epic, 20, 128
episode, 22, 74, 85
equipment, 29, 117, 135, 144–146, 148–149,
151, 153, 164
equivalent, 50, 167

Erik, 66
especially, 135, 151, 193
essay, 50
Esselstyn, 94
Esselystyn, 94
essential, 175, 177
essentially, 43, 51, 61, 114, 117, 160
establish, 52, 76, 85, 102, 157, 172
established, 59–60, 102, 163, 182, 190
establishing, 76, 178
estimate, 101, 144
estimating, 146
etcetera, 132, 155, 171, 192
ethical, 42

ethics, 46, 88
ethnic, 43, 49, 51, 55, 57, 71, 91–92
ethnicity, 71
ethnofiction, 55
ethnographic, 54–57
ethnography, 55, 104
Eugene, 87
Europe, 18
European, 55, 91–92
evidence, 64, 75–76, 78, 95, 102–103, 109
evil, 49, 102
evolution, 72, 106, 110
evolutionary, 45
evolve, 21, 106, 190
evolved, 23, 28, 63, 78, 106
expected, 174

experiment, 191
exploration, 17, 27, 49, 80, 103, 111,
128–130, 136
explore, 18–20, 38–39, 44, 46, 50, 54, 57–59,
62, 68, 71–72, 75, 78–79, 82, 87–88, 93,
96, 101, 103, 106, 108–109, 111, 113,
116, 121, 123, 129–130, 187
explored, 18, 41–42, 66, 82, 97, 109, 120,
131, 133
exploring, 25, 37, 73, 92, 102, 113, 130
exterior, 165, 174–175
extremist, 42
eyewitness, 44, 76

F

facilitate, 27, 44, 82, 130, 164, 173, 180–181,
190–192
factual, 29, 72, 91, 194
Fahrenheit, 23, 87
Fairey, 59–60
fans, 69
Farina, 85
farm, 28, 117–118
farmer, 46, 141
farming, 47
farther, 112
fast, 32, 76, 105, 161
faster, 74, 161
father, 62, 80

faux, 20, 121
favor, 160
FDR, 43
feature, 20, 23, 25, 40, 46, 55, 58, 71, 77, 97, 110, 133
featured, 29
featuring, 19, 132
fed, 93
feedback, 55, 194
Fegruson, 87
feigned, 42
female, 101–103, 110, 113
fences, 47
festival, 63, 132, 196
fibula, 40
fiction, 19, 23–26, 35, 37, 43–44, 52, 58, 67,
119–123, 128, 135–136, 144, 159, 166,
185, 191, 195
fictional, 20, 39, 41, 44, 48–50, 68, 118–122,
136
fiction project, 141
fifteen, 40
fifty, 22, 32, 36, 41, 95, 124
fighters, 96
fighting, 40–42, 195
fill, 156, 159, 165, 174–176
filled, 114
film, 17–18, 20–33, 35, 37–39, 42–44, 46,
48–53, 55–59, 61–63, 65–66, 68–74, 76,
78–85, 87, 89, 92–95, 99–100, 102,

BIBLIOGRAPHY AND INDEX

104–110, 112–124, 127–129, 132–136,
139, 141–148, 150–151, 155, 159–161,
164–166, 172, 174, 176–177, 180,
185–190, 193–196
filmed, 84, 96
filming, 41, 55, 70–72, 130, 190
filmmaker, 17–19, 21–25, 27–29, 31, 38,
41–42, 45–48, 51, 53, 55–58, 60–61, 67,
69–70, 74, 76–77, 82–84, 90–91, 94, 96,
98, 100, 106, 115–116, 120, 123–124,
126, 134–135, 143–144, 151, 155, 180,
185, 188, 196
Filmmakers, 36, 120, 143
filmmaking, 17, 23, 28–29, 50, 63, 100, 115,
145, 159
Films, 19–20, 22, 72, 80, 87, 108, 123, 160
filter, 46–48, 148, 174, 177, 195
filtered, 177
filtering, 44
finance, 91
financing, 24, 150–152
fingers, 68
fire, 40–41, 55, 96

firefights, 36
firsthand, 80, 129

fish, 76, 149
Fisher, 110
fit, 34, 61–62, 72–73, 78, 91, 97, 100, 109,
130, 135, 174
five, 46, 79, 94, 113–114
fixed, 166
Flaherty, 55, 120
flash, 186, 193
flat, 38, 70
flex, 174–175
Flexfills, 165
Flint, 23
floats, 162
Florentine, 22
Florida, 109
flow, 115, 124, 186
flowing, 62
fluid, 58, 114, 145
fluorescent, 156, 175–177
fly, 18, 59, 69, 93, 157
focal, 143, 163, 166–167
focus, 18, 57, 62–63, 83, 90, 96, 121,
128–129, 155, 166, 170, 173
focused, 166
focuses, 52, 64, 81
focusing, 57
Fog, 50–51, 88, 90
foggy, 109
Folkerson, 94
folklore, 37
followed, 24, 157, 166
food, 94–95, 123, 152
foot, 36, 41
footage, 20, 26, 31, 40–41, 46–47,

50–51, 55,
57–61, 63, 65–66, 68–70, 72, 76,
82–83,
85–89, 101, 105, 107, 110–112,
121, 123,
134–138, 141, 143, 150, 154, 156,
158,
164, 178–179, 183, 185–187, 192
foreground, 173
foreign, 131
foreshadowing, 71
foreshadows, 124
Forks, 94–95
format, 19–20, 28, 30, 38–39, 57,
63, 75,
109, 111, 113–115, 118–119,
121, 123,
131, 135–136, 138–139, 141,
146,
160–161, 166–167, 186–187
Formats, 135
formatted, 140
formatting, 141
forty, 63, 65, 91
four, 71, 84–86, 95, 99, 105, 113,
174, 176,
192
fourteen, 97
Fox, 99–100
fps, 176–177
fracking, 98–99
fracture, 99
fracturing, 99, 101
fragments, 28
frame, 61, 70, 73–74, 160,
162–163, 167,
172–174, 181–182, 187, 189
framework, 134
framing, 163, 171
Fran, 24
France, 37, 59, 93, 102
Francisco, 69, 89
Franklin, 49
Fred, 28, 67, 117
Frederick, 93, 126
free, 69, 71, 75, 91, 93, 99
freelance, 22
French, 50
Frenchman, 59
Frieda, 23
friend, 46, 52, 78, 85–86, 132,
193
friendly, 28, 43, 117
front, 44, 70, 101, 110, 116–117,
123, 166,
176, 181
FS, 162, 168
further, 53
Fury, 95–97

G

Gabriela, 76
gaffer, 148–149, 153
gage, 142
gain, 41, 84
gallery, 60, 116
game, 52, 65, 97–98, 120, 181
Garden, 70
Gardner, 56
gas, 98–99, 101
Gasland, 98–100

gasoline, 98
gather, 102
gathering, 134, 156, 159
Geeta, 57
Gelb, 79
gels, 174, 177
gender, 43, 101
generalizations, 103
generation, 37, 57, 85
generational, 97
generously, 75
genetic, 75
genre, 18, 54, 63, 100, 122
gENRES, 54
Geoff, 61
Geographic, 23, 75, 111
Geography, 71
George, 62, 85–86, 108
Gerald, 74
German, 49–50
gestalt, 74
giant, 23, 112
Gilkey, 90
Gimme Shelter, 69
glass, 79, 89, 100, 173
Goddess, 102–103
Goebbels, 109
gorillas, 77
government, 28, 43, 49, 77, 87, 91, 96, 100, 118, 131, 133, 142
Governor, 85
graduate, 23–24, 113
graffiti, 39, 59–60
Graham, 110
gramophone, 55

grandfather, 62
Grandmother, 96
grandparents, 96
grant, 71, 90
graphic, 19, 31, 39, 51, 87, 93, 95, 101–102, 105, 108, 111, 150, 174
Greece, 52
Greek, 118
green, 90–91, 134, 143
Greg, 108
grew, 29, 99
grey, 141–142
Grierson, 42, 80
grip, 40, 151–152
Grips, 151
guerilla, 100
Guetta, 59
Guggenheim, 68, 75–76
Guinea, 56
guitar, 68
guitarists, 68

H

Hajian, 115
Hampshire, 22
handheld, 67, 100, 149, 159
handicapped, 96
handicaps, 93
handing, 37
Hannus, 50
harassment, 91
Harlan, 82–84
Harman, 105
Harmony, 60

Harris, 66
Harvest, 28, 117
hate, 86–87
hatred, 49
haven, 97
Hawkins, 66
HD, 161, 167, 172, 174
Headquarters, 41
health, 42, 65, 93–94
healthcare, 93
healthy, 95
Heartherten, 36
Heather, 95–96
heinous, 86
Heinzerling, 64
Hell, 70
help, 19, 34, 40, 48, 64, 67, 71, 78, 85–88,
90, 92, 129, 133, 136–137, 144, 148–149,
151, 154, 156, 159, 164, 173–175, 185,
188, 190–191, 195–196
helped, 43, 78, 80
helping, 68, 148
Henry, 51
Herdy, 101
Herzog, 37–38, 58, 123–124
Hetherington, 40–41
hide, 123
Higgins, 114–115
high, 24, 29, 90, 97–98, 101, 104, 113–114,
146–147, 157, 160, 174, 176, 195
higher, 67, 101, 160, 164

highlight, 66, 157
highlighted, 20, 73, 94
highly, 24, 143
Hill, 110
hired, 83, 143–144, 150, 153
Hiro, 67
historian, 32, 49, 73, 92, 102, 133
historic, 31–32, 90, 109
historical, 26, 31, 35, 50–51, 72, 82, 88, 90,
102, 112, 119–121, 132, 147, 151, 194
historically, 72, 87, 120
history, 19, 21–23, 32–34, 50, 55, 61–62,
71–73, 75, 83–85, 88–89, 91–93, 97,
102–103, 108, 110–111, 129
Hollywood, 105
holocaust, 50
homemade, 106
Homes, 85
Homo sapien, 106
Honor, 20, 121
Hopper, 31
horror, 50
horse, 107
hospital, 93, 104–105
host, 19, 28, 66, 93, 123
housing, 80, 90
Houston, 112
human, 18, 30, 37, 43–45, 48–51, 54–55, 59,
71, 75–76, 78–80, 92, 127, 167, 171
humanistic, 42, 84, 107

humanities, 71
humanity, 38, 50, 54, 71–72, 91
humanizes, 112
humankind, 112
humans, 37–38, 47, 76–79, 86, 106, 117
humor, 43
hunted, 76
hunting, 37, 55, 120
hurt, 83
Huxley, 106
hybrid, 19, 23, 26, 57, 63, 105, 120, 123
hydraulic, 99, 101
hygiene, 93
hypertension, 94

I

idea, 17, 27, 43–44, 56, 58–59, 61, 87, 103,
106, 121, 127–134, 138, 142, 146, 148,
154, 157, 171, 173, 179–180, 185, 187–189, 194, 196
ideology, 20, 48, 121, 131
illegal, 81
Illinois, 71
illness, 30, 93
illuminate, 68
illuminated, 60
illumination, 148
illusion, 58, 160
image, 27, 62, 148–149, 159–161, 167–168
imagery, 117
imaginable, 20
imaginary, 182
imagine, 41, 54, 132
imagined, 130
IMDB, 53
immigrant, 57, 91–92, 133
Immigrants, 91–92
immigration, 92, 133
implant, 96
INDB, 76
independent, 60, 90–91, 94, 131, 150
India, 57, 80
indigenous, 77, 124
indoctrination, 48
industrial, 116–117, 122, 139
industry, 17, 62, 71, 99, 109–110
inferior, 49
Inferno, 123
infomercials, 118
informational, 48, 118, 120, 122, 139
institution, 20, 93, 121, 131
instruction, 158
instrument, 63, 149, 176, 186
insurance, 146
insure, 136–138, 147, 166
intellectual, 143
Intercutting, 181
interior, 38, 175
internal, 48, 118, 163
international, 71, 87, 113
internationally, 28, 58, 76
Internet, 33, 131, 146
interview, 18–20, 28–29, 31–33, 35, 38,
40–41, 43, 49–50, 52–54, 58–59,

61–63,
66, 68–69, 72, 75–76, 79, 81, 84–87,
89–90, 92–93, 95, 97, 100–102, 104,
107–108, 110–111, 115, 120–122,
129–130, 132, 135–138, 145, 153–154,
156, 159, 162–164, 171–172, 175–176,
178, 182–183, 186–187, 189, 191–193,
195–196
interviewee, 54, 62, 77, 130, 137–138, 145,
151, 162–164, 166, 171–172, 183, 191
Interviewees, 181
interviewer, 33, 54, 58, 87, 151, 162,
171–172, 182
interviews, 19, 33, 38, 77, 90, 108, 115, 119,
152, 175, 193
Inuit, 55, 120
investigative, 28, 43, 101, 118
invitation, 157
invited, 188
involve, 27, 77, 100, 186
iPhone, 34
iris, 174
Irish, 91
irony, 43
Island, 106
Israel, 47
Israeli, 46
issued, 109
ISSUES, 93, 98, 101
Italian, 22, 91
Italy, 41

J

Jack, 68
Jackson, 61, 86
Jacques, 23
Jagger, 70, 111
jailed, 86
James, 71, 86, 90
Japan, 64–65, 76
Japanese, 43, 79, 92
Jarecki, 87
Jason, 110
jazz, 72–75, 161
Jean, 50
Jeff, 62
Jennifer, 115
Jessie, 86
Jews, 49
Jimmy, 68
Jiro, 79–80
Joan, 84–85
jock, 53
Joe, 52, 67, 111
Joesph, 109
Johansoon, 61
John, 20, 42, 66, 80, 89, 93, 121
Johnson, 89–90
Jones, 23
Joni, 66
Joseph, 28, 118

Josh, 95, 99–100
journalism, 21
journalist, 41, 47, 130
journalistic, 19, 23, 29, 54, 77, 88, 117
Journalists, 101
journals, 32, 122
Judith, 56, 110
juncture, 83
Junger, 36, 40–41
just, 39, 59, 62, 64, 85, 99, 101, 107, 110, 112, 115–116, 127, 178, 180, 188
juxtaposition, 51

K

Kalyanee, 87
Kane, 108
Karda, 112
Karen, 88
Kargman, 113–115
Kate, 115
Katrina, 24
Kazuo, 43
Ken Burns, 22, 25, 31, 49, 72, 74–75, 89, 92, 115, 122
Kennedy, 62, 89
Kentucky, 83
Kerry, 20, 121
Kevin, 110
Kiev, 123
Kilgallen, 61
King, 86, 88
Klan, 85
Klauber, 110

Knives, 94–95
knowing, 77, 186
knowledgable, 187
Kolkata, 80–81
Kopple, 82–84
Korengal, 36, 40
Korine, 61
Kornengal, 41
Kovacs, 67
Kurosawa, 43
Kyo, 43

L

LA, 59
landscape, 115–117, 138–139, 171, 190
Landscapes, 115–117
Laslo, 67
latitude, 38
lava, 124
law, 23, 30, 91–92, 98, 141–143, 164
Lawyer, 143
layer, 53, 56, 67, 176
layman, 142
layout, 139
LCD, 160
Leadership, 86
learn, 17, 24, 47, 63, 74, 79, 88, 90, 107, 130
learning, 80, 82, 84, 90, 96, 113
lecture, 160
Lee, 23–24, 62, 85–86, 94
legal, 108, 142
lens, 54, 56, 81, 156–157, 163, 166–168, 170

lenses, 148, 159, 166–167
Leon, 102
lessons, 88
letter, 49–50, 72, 122
Levees, 24
Lewis, 56, 108
Li, 91–92
liability, 146
liberated, 50
liberation, 83
library, 39, 143
license, 58, 123
lie, 20, 109, 121
Liebowitz, 24
lifestyles, 95
Lin, 23
Lindsay, 97
linear, 61, 160, 192
lion, 107
Lisa, 110
list, 53, 132, 134–136, 138, 142, 152, 178
listen, 33, 130, 137, 179, 189, 194
listened, 74
listener, 74
listening, 66, 135, 137, 157, 179–180, 183, 192
literature, 35, 71, 106
Lobby, 131
lobbyists, 131
Locations, 152
Log, 148–149, 186
logged, 138, 148
logistics, 147, 155
Lois, 62, 83
London, 63
Lorenz, 49
Louis, 39, 53, 90
love, 22, 30, 65, 68, 79, 99, 110
loved, 33
Lowe, 28, 117
LS, 162, 168
Lucy, 103
Lumière, 28, 38–39, 53, 122
Luther, 86, 111
Luxembourg, 30
lying, 82
lynching, 75
Lyndon, 90
Lynn, 105

M

MacDougall, 56
Machiko, 43
Madison, 70
Magaret, 61
magazine, 23, 29–30, 33, 35
Maher, 94
mainstream, 60
majority, 109, 131
making, 17–18, 23–25, 48, 59, 74, 79–81,
83–84, 90, 93, 95, 103–104, 106, 120,
130–131, 149, 152, 158, 161
male, 86, 113
maltreatment, 93
mammals, 76
mammoth, 117
Manassas, 97
manifests, 64

manipulate, 44–45, 48, 92, 109
manipulated, 19, 120, 130
manipulating, 131
manipulation, 44
Manufactured, 115–117
manufacturing, 115, 118
Mari, 96
Marianne, 96
Marquette, 67
Marsh, 110
Marshal, 93
Marten, 63
Martin, 24, 31, 66, 71, 86, 90, 97
Mary, 62
Masayuki, 43
Massachusetts, 22, 93
master, 79, 162
Matt, 87
Maya, 23
Maybury, 56
Mayes, 22
Maysles, 69
McCarthy, 28, 118
McCullough, 22
McDonalds, 123
McFetridge, 61
McGee, 61
McLuhan, 160–161
McNair, 85
McNamara, 88–89
McTaggart, 105
MCU, 168
me, 23, 65, 106, 123
meals, 153, 155
media, 30, 35, 108
mediaocracy, 108

medical, 93, 96, 101
medicine, 43, 54
medium, 18, 30, 34–35, 39, 51, 54, 56, 72,
108–109, 116, 127, 131, 148, 159–161,
168, 180
mediums, 17, 74, 134, 172
Meehl, 107
member, 25, 32, 48, 52, 55, 66, 85, 90, 144,
151, 158, 162, 178
memorabilia, 34
Memphis, 97
mental, 93
mentally, 93, 113
methodology, 159
methods, 18, 34, 107, 120, 142, 159, 165
metropolitan, 80, 90
MFA, 24
Michael, 23, 42, 87, 93, 100, 108, 123
Michale, 67
Michele, 95
Michigan, 23
Mick, 69–70, 111
microphone, 149–150
middle, 51, 53, 61, 95, 100, 128, 132–133,
163, 178–179, 187
Midler, 111
midst, 84
Mifune, 43
migrant, 28, 117–118
migrate, 91

Mike, 61
military, 40, 46, 101–102, 113
militias, 77
millimeters, 166
million, 30, 50, 80, 95, 101
Mills, 61
mind, 44–45, 48, 87–88, 117, 124, 129, 137,
157
minded, 106
mindfully, 48
miner, 80, 82–84
miniaturized, 29
mining, 84, 116
minstrelsy, 75
minute, 20, 22, 31, 34, 39, 41, 50, 53, 59, 61,
63, 72, 74, 76, 87, 90, 98, 100, 110, 115,
152, 178
Missile, 89
Mitchell, 66
mitigate, 48
mix, 61, 115, 190, 194–195
mixed, 35, 175, 190
mixer, 149, 153, 157–158
mixing, 149, 190, 195
mixture, 19, 83, 90, 99
Miyagawa, 43
mm, 22, 29, 160, 166–167, 174
mob, 70
mobile, 165
Mock, 23
MOCKUMENTARY, 20, 121
modern, 29–30, 45, 53, 55–56, 58, 80, 108,
174, 180
modular, 45
modulating, 150
module, 45, 112
Monastery, 123
money, 64, 95, 108, 160
monitor, 150, 158, 174, 188
Monks, 123
montage, 31–32, 50–51, 81, 89, 95, 117
moon, 111–112
Moore, 23, 42–43, 87, 93, 100, 108, 123
morality, 76
Morgan, 110
Mori, 43
Morris, 88–89, 119
Morrison, 66
mortality, 95
mother, 23, 81, 96, 102–103, 112
motion, 38, 53, 116, 180, 191
motorcycle, 63
movie, 22, 161
ms, 101, 162–163
MSNBC, 117
Muddy, 66–67
multicolumn, 141
multicultural, 71
multimedia, 17, 33, 35, 113, 123, 136, 139
multiple, 56, 65, 78, 131, 137–138, 140,
189–190, 194
Murrow, 28, 117
museum, 30, 35, 98, 116
music, 32–33, 50, 57–59, 63,

65–69, 71–75,
82, 86, 88–89, 92, 98, 108–112, 115,
123–124, 150, 161, 186, 188–190, 194–195
musical, 65–66, 72, 186, 195
musician, 27, 66, 68–70, 73, 75, 186
mutters, 86
Myers, 67
myriad, 122

N

Nanook, 55, 120
Narita, 67
narrate, 19, 43, 89, 99, 115
narrated, 28, 31, 64–65, 117
narration, 26, 28, 32–33, 50, 81, 87, 92, 108,
111–112, 120, 135, 147, 187
narrative, 19, 22, 33, 42–43, 58, 68, 98, 104,
107, 109, 119–120, 134, 184, 186–187
Narratives, 18
narrator, 59, 72, 123, 135
NASA, 111
national, 23, 32–33, 71, 73, 75, 77, 102, 109, 111
nationally, 28, 72, 90, 117
nature, 19, 31, 34, 39, 44, 48, 54, 58, 75–78,
87, 104, 106, 111–112, 122, 143
negative, 65, 129, 173
negatively, 42
neglected, 64, 75

NEH, 71
neighbor, 37, 46, 48
neighborhood, 71–72, 97
Neil, 66, 112
Neolithic, 37
Netflix, 77
Neuman, 65
neutral, 57, 163, 171
neutralize, 54
Neville, 110
News, 159
newscast, 172
newscaster, 159, 172
newspaper, 30, 32–33, 35, 85–86, 142
NFB, 32
Nick, 114
Nicola, 110
night, 40, 50–51, 60, 83, 97, 175
nightlife, 98
nightly, 47, 84
nine, 22, 79, 81
nineteen, 65, 72–73
ninety, 20, 41, 59, 61, 72, 95, 104, 110, 115
nomads, 37
nominated, 22, 32, 40, 46, 53, 72, 77, 98
Nominee, 101
nonfiction, 17–20, 24–26, 28, 30, 35, 38–39,
44–45, 48, 50–52, 58, 63, 75, 88–89, 91,
100, 104, 114, 118–123, 127–129,
135–136, 138–139, 144, 147,

151, 164,
166, 172, 187
Norika, 63–65
North, 55, 120, 129
notable, 105
notice, 142, 161
notion, 18, 28, 84, 88, 90, 97, 102, 128, 130,
134, 142
notoriety, 61
nouveau, 105
nova, 78, 111
novel, 106, 108, 128
now, 22, 24, 37, 47, 51, 63–64, 68, 74, 77, 94, 96, 107, 110, 160–161
NPR, 33
NTSC, 177
NYC, 64–65
NYU, 24

O

Obama, 95
Obesity, 95
objective, 29, 40, 42, 44–45, 47, 49, 51, 56,
87, 109
objectivity, 42, 58, 84
observational, 18, 29, 115
observations, 106, 128
observe, 29, 46–47, 117
observed, 34, 38–39, 44, 84, 183
observer, 34, 55, 69, 83, 114–115, 163
observing, 93, 115–116
ocean, 47, 112
offenders, 102

offer, 18, 29–30, 35, 47, 74, 87, 90, 99–100,
103, 105, 114, 122, 164–165, 186
offered, 76, 122, 142
offering, 122
office, 123, 152, 154, 164, 175–176
Offices, 164, 177
official, 100, 116
Ohms, 164
oil, 77
OK, 41
Olympic, 52
online, 129, 186, 196
Ono, 79
opera, 124
optical, 148
optically, 167
oral, 32–34, 97
Orca, 76
orchestra, 27, 124
Orleans, 72–73
Orwell, 108–109
Orwellian, 108
Oscar, 53, 77, 97, 110
Ossie, 86
osteoporosis, 94
OTS, 168
outcomes, 87, 100
overall, 63, 114, 116, 148, 156, 165, 177
own, 22, 24, 29, 37, 42–43, 46–48, 56, 60,
64, 68, 79–81, 98, 117, 124, 131, 134, 158
owned, 142

owner, 79, 83, 138, 141, 145

P
pace, 52, 61, 73–74, 82, 92, 98, 107,
115–116, 192
paced, 32, 60, 68, 76, 87, 100, 105–106, 161
pacing, 51, 128, 150, 186, 188–189, 191
painting, 31, 37–38, 57, 64, 102
PAINTINGS, 31
Pakistan, 40
PAL, 176
Palast, 108
Palestinian, 46–47
pan, 180–181
Panetta, 102
panoramic, 159
Pappas, 108
parade, 75, 162, 178
paradox, 75
parallel, 51, 68–69, 71–73, 77, 95, 100–101,
110, 176, 187, 192
paralleled, 46, 100
Pare, 49
parent, 47, 57, 85, 95–96, 113
park, 76–77, 157, 165
parodies, 142
part, 27–28, 31, 34, 42, 46, 55, 62, 71, 74,
91, 102, 104, 106, 120, 128, 130, 136,
145, 161, 174, 178–180, 185–186,

188–190, 192, 195
partial, 119
partially, 31, 188
Patel, 57
path, 24, 28, 52, 92
patients, 93
patrol, 36, 40–41
Paul, 66
payroll, 151
PBS, 72, 78, 91, 111
Pechersk, 123
Pennsylvania, 99
Pennybacker, 29
People, 83, 182
peoples, 55
Peralta, 23
perform, 68, 70, 149, 151–152
performance, 55, 65–69, 109–110, 114–115
performed, 58, 68, 123
performers, 67, 114
performing, 67, 70, 114
period, 40, 46, 63, 102, 120, 145
permission, 56, 71, 141–142, 145
permitted, 81, 141, 166
Peter, 96
phenomenon, 44
Philip, 79, 89
philosophers, 45
philosophical, 44, 104
Philosophically, 44
philosophy, 28, 45, 63, 71, 98, 107
photo, 30, 38, 56
photograph, 22, 30–32, 34, 39, 50, 56–58,
63, 72, 79, 81, 85–86, 90, 92, 97,

107,
109, 111, 116, 122, 136, 143, 160, 183,
190
photographed, 115
photographer, 30, 81, 173
photographic, 29, 31, 134, 173, 190
photographically, 81
Photographs, 30, 71
photography, 22, 26, 30, 34, 38, 47, 67, 82,
114, 116, 144, 146, 148–149, 151–153,
156, 160, 166
photojournalism, 29
Photoshop, 186
physical, 53
physically, 113, 167
picture, 30, 38, 53, 56, 74, 81, 85, 135–136,
138, 140–141, 154, 160, 175, 180, 187,
191
pistol, 70
plagues, 102
planet, 75–76, 112
platform, 53, 178–179
platoon, 40–42
playing, 68, 70, 97, 100, 188
plenty, 140
plight, 84
plot, 26, 51, 67
Plow, 49
poachers, 77
pocket, 30, 143

pod, 33
podium, 156
poet, 58, 105
poetry, 58
polar, 149–150
polarized, 88
police, 44, 84–85, 96
policy, 20, 88, 121, 133
political, 20, 28, 34, 39, 43, 45, 48–49, 71,
80, 82, 87–88, 90, 108, 121, 131–132, 163
politician, 20, 92, 121, 179
politics, 19, 41, 71–73, 87–88, 91–92, 96, 133
Pollard, 85
polluting, 99
Pont, 37
portrait, 34, 63, 81, 107, 138–139
pose, 56, 108
position, 26, 29, 57, 113–115, 121, 147–150,
152, 155, 178–180
positioned, 163
positioning, 149
positive, 65, 82, 129, 131, 173
post, 55, 101, 105, 186, 191
posters, 163
postproduction, 144, 158, 185
posture, 18
POV, 39–40, 100, 163
poverty, 80
power, 35, 61, 83, 148–149
powerful, 84, 102
practical, 136, 189–190
Pray, 62–63

predators, 101
prehistoric, 103
prehistory, 102
preliminary, 114, 129–130, 134
Premier, 95, 186
Premiere, 186
premixing, 195
prepared, 156
prepares, 194
preproduction, 67, 127, 137, 143–144, 152
prerogatives, 26, 46
presence, 60, 92, 190, 194–195
present, 39, 44–45, 51, 54, 62, 68, 75–76,
82, 99, 101–103, 108–110, 135, 160
presentation, 30, 35, 39, 74–75, 104, 113,
119, 134, 172
PRESENTATIONS, 35
presented, 29–30, 32, 49, 61, 75, 86, 94,
103–104, 109, 131, 134
presenting, 38, 117
preserve, 54–55, 58, 71, 77, 193
President, 20, 43, 75, 89, 121
press, 143, 178
preview, 196
previewed, 72
previous, 70, 83
previously, 33, 72, 97, 115, 129, 161, 181, 191
previsualize, 127
prices, 98
primal, 48

primary, 29, 178
prime, 167, 195
primitive, 55
print, 131, 143, 160
printed, 152
priority, 45, 47, 56, 91, 150, 156–157, 192
Prix, 113
procreation, 45, 48
produce, 25, 33, 58, 68, 86, 118, 140, 144
produced, 17, 28, 30, 33, 50, 56, 72, 88, 111,
117, 146, 160
producer, 23, 25–27, 143–144, 146–147,
150–153, 155, 185, 196
Producers, 151
producing, 160
production, 17–18, 21–22, 25–27, 30, 35, 75,
118–119, 128, 136, 143–148, 150–152,
155, 157–159, 166–167, 174, 191, 196
Productions, 23
profession, 21, 113
professional, 19, 43, 93, 97, 141, 167,
194–195
professionally, 57, 156
Professor, 38, 58, 73, 104
profiles, 34, 63, 107
program, 28, 75, 111, 120, 134, 141, 178,
186, 191

229

programmed, 47
prohibition, 92
project, 17, 25–27, 33, 38, 60–61, 66, 71, 90–91, 122–123, 133–134, 136–139, 143–144, 146–147, 150–151, 175, 185–187, 195
projected, 100, 160, 188
projection, 161
projectors, 161
PROJECTS, 27, 127
promote, 48–49, 102, 131, 196
propaganda, 20, 44, 48–49, 91, 121, 131
propagandist, 88
property, 143, 145, 148
props, 151
proscenium, 180
prostitutes, 81
protagonist, 52, 132
protesters, 46
protests, 46, 86
PSA, 118
psychological, 93
psychologists, 44–45, 97
publications, 142
pundits, 47
punk, 60

Q
Quad, 52
Quadriplegic, 52
quantitative, 160
quest, 52, 98, 100, 105, 123
quietly, 165
quote, 58, 74, 94, 108–109, 136, 142

R
race, 73, 75, 192–193
racial, 49, 73, 92
racism, 48, 73, 85–86
racist, 85, 92
Raconteurs, 68
radio, 32–33, 160
railroad, 91
raise, 21, 64, 87, 177
raised, 21
rally, 156, 163, 178
random, 59
range, 55, 93
rangers, 77
Ranks, 101
rape, 101
rashomon, 43–44
ratio, 174, 176
Ravi, 57
Ray, 67, 111
reconstruct, 154
recreate, 19, 31, 39, 60, 158
recreated, 120, 122
reenact, 119
reenacted, 105
reenactments, 50, 89, 118–120, 151
reference, 20, 31, 92, 181
Reflectors, 174
refugee, 77
rehearsals, 114

rehearsed, 38, 166
rehearsing, 58, 166
Reinert, 111
religion, 43, 49, 71, 102–104, 192
religious, 48–49, 86, 103–105, 124
religiously, 106
replica, 31
report, 35, 101, 149, 151
reporter, 19, 43, 123
reporting, 29, 49, 77, 172
Requiem, 124
require, 25, 27, 48, 116, 129, 136–137, 145–146, 158, 161–166, 170–171, 181, 189, 192, 195
required, 24, 36, 41, 83, 135, 144–148, 150, 152, 165, 172, 188
rescued, 77
research, 25–26, 28, 71, 78, 94, 118, 128–132, 134, 147, 152
researched, 138
researchers, 95
researching, 127–129, 131
resident, 46, 71–72, 77, 100
Residents, 100
Resnais, 50–51
Restrepo, 36, 40–41
Retrepo, 36
review, 17, 124, 142, 146, 157, 186–187, 194, 196
reviewed, 57, 188

Reviews, 124
rhetoric, 92
rhythm, 58, 116, 150, 186, 190
Ric, 91–92
rich, 62, 104–105
Richard, 85
riche, 105
rifles, 55, 120
rig, 149, 156
Rights, 84
rigors, 113
Ringo, 66
River, 49
Roadie, 63
Robbie, 66
Robert, 29, 55–56, 88–89, 108, 120
Robertson, 66, 85
Robinson, 62
rock, 36, 41, 65, 99
Roger, 22–23
Roma, 49
Ron, 66
Ronnie, 66
Roosevelt, 43, 49
rough, 34, 188
route, 37
Rubin, 51
rude, 40
rugby, 52
ruins, 118
rule, 88, 115, 142, 166
Rumble, 68
Rumspringa, 103–104
runner, 193
Rush, 91

Russian, 28
Rutman, 58

S

Saint, 90
sales, 38, 69, 122, 139
Salesman, 69
salvage, 55, 104, 116
Sam, 85
sanctuaries, 76
Sandburg, 30
Sanders, 108
sanitation, 93
sapiens, 106
satirical, 20, 121, 142
saturation, 159
scale, 31
scape, 31
scene, 19, 31–32, 40, 52, 54–55, 58, 64, 67, 69–70, 83–84, 86, 89, 94, 100, 105, 107, 109, 115–117, 119, 124, 132, 135–137, 148–150, 154, 157–159, 162–163, 165, 168, 177–179, 181, 186–188, 190–193, 195
scenery, 151
scenes, 162, 166, 193
schedule, 26, 144–146
scheduling, 135, 147, 151
Schmeer, 88

scholar, 72, 108
scholarly, 118, 142
scholarships, 114
school, 22–24, 59, 97–98, 113, 118
Schuler, 67
science, 19, 38, 54, 71–72, 78, 106, 111
sciences, 71
scientific, 75–76, 79, 111, 151
scientists, 79, 105, 129
SCLC, 86
score, 27, 58, 65, 79, 107, 112, 115, 186
Scorsese, 24, 66–67
Scott, 83
scout, 26, 146, 149, 165
scouting, 151
Scratch, 63
screened, 55, 63, 118, 160, 188, 194
screening, 58, 129, 188, 194–196
SCREENINGS, 193, 196
screenplay, 135–136
script, 25–27, 39, 67, 111, 123, 132–141, 144–148, 150, 152, 155, 157, 183, 186–188, 194–195
scripted, 19, 52, 119, 136–137, 178
scripting, 141
sculpture, 64, 102
sea, 76
seamless, 165
seamlessly, 154
Sean, 67
Sebastian, 36, 40–41
Secretary, 89, 102

secular, 103
security, 43, 77, 104, 179
segment, 66, 69, 110, 119, 136, 142, 186, 188
segregated, 85
segregation, 73
self, 45, 91, 105, 116, 185, 194
selfie, 34
seminar, 90, 160
Senate, 28
Senator, 20, 28, 118, 121
sense, 25, 32, 43, 61, 66, 76, 89, 96, 133, 160, 163, 179, 182
sensitivity, 113
sensory, 116
sentence, 133
September, 84, 86
sequence, 78, 89, 116, 150, 183, 192
sequential, 160
series, 23, 72, 78, 91, 102, 111, 145, 157, 166
service, 93–94, 96, 118, 186, 195
serving, 101
session, 68–69, 194
set, 29, 31, 41, 64, 67, 87–89, 105, 119–120, 137, 144–145, 147, 150, 153, 157–158, 164, 166, 175, 179–180, 189, 195
setting, 57, 67, 116, 148–149, 151, 157, 171, 190
settlements, 46
settlers, 46

setup, 57, 145
sex, 81, 102
sexual, 101
sexuality, 102
Shadyac, 104–105
Shepard, 59–60
Sherman, 22
shifting, 117
Shimizu, 65
Shin, 91–92
Shine, 24, 160
Shinohara, 63–65
ship, 112, 116, 155
shirt, 115, 177
Shoes, 63
shoot, 22, 25, 27, 56, 59, 67, 134–135, 137–138, 144, 146, 149, 158, 162, 175–176, 178–179, 182–183
shooting, 25–27, 38, 46, 56, 67, 81, 100, 104, 132, 134–139, 141, 144–149, 152–154, 161, 164, 174, 176–177, 179, 181, 186–187
shooting script, 141
showcase, 24
Shui, 32
siblings, 85, 95
Sicko, 23, 42, 93
sign, 26, 157, 163, 178–180
Silver, 63
simulated, 172
simulation, 111
simultaneous, 56, 161
singer, 66, 110

singing, 86, 123
sites, 34, 99
sitting, 54, 59, 89, 162–163, 171, 182
situation, 40–41, 44–45, 49, 77, 116, 130, 141, 145, 148, 154, 156–158, 163–165,

171, 175–178, 182, 189, 194
Siverstein, 62
skateboarder, 23
skateboarding, 60
slide, 30, 39, 75, 100, 134
snapshot, 30
Soares, 52
social, 21, 24, 34, 38, 42–43, 45, 55, 71–72, 80, 82, 87–88, 96–97, 107, 109, 121, 128–129, 132–133
socialism, 43
socialized, 43
socially, 72, 87
society, 55, 72, 103
sociological, 60
sociologist, 133
software, 141, 186, 189, 194–195
SOHO, 77
soldier, 40–42, 50, 77, 122
solution, 43, 76, 82, 87, 90, 105, 121–122, 177, 182
sound, 27, 53, 62, 72, 74, 82, 85–87, 89, 95–97, 100, 108, 115, 124, 127, 149–150, 153, 160, 178–179, 189–190, 194–195
source, 35, 50, 57, 91, 98, 111, 121, 124, 129–131, 148, 150, 174–176, 190
Southeast, 71
southern, 37, 77, 86
speaker, 68, 156, 163, 178–180, 188
speaking, 24, 80, 93, 108, 112, 163, 172, 182
species, 78
speculation, 50, 103, 119
speculative, 103, 119
Spike Lee, 24, 85–86
spin, 48, 109
Spinal, 20, 121
spiritual, 103
spirituality, 102–103
splicing, 186, 189
splitting, 189
spokesperson, 45
sponsored, 49, 63, 96, 102, 118
spontaneous, 33, 49, 100, 166
sport, 52–54, 97, 113
Springsteen, 110–111
Squires, 22
Stacy, 23
stage, 38, 67–68, 70, 114–115, 132, 141, 166, 179–180, 182
staged, 18, 120, 122, 130
staging, 39, 55, 58, 104, 166
stalk, 101
stance, 113
standby, 178

standpoint, 29, 63, 147, 166
Stardom, 109–110
stars, 43
static, 116, 149, 157, 162, 178, 180
station, 79
statistics, 62, 108
statuettes, 103
Steadicam, 149
Steeplechase, 91
Steichen, 30
Stephe, 61
stereotypes, 97
Steve, 31
Stevie, 111
STILLS, 196
stimulus, 160–161
Sting, 111
stock, 26, 143, 146, 150, 174, 177
storefront, 60
Stories, 79, 128
storyboard, 67, 136, 138–139, 157
storyteller, 44–45, 51, 128
storytelling, 17, 25, 29, 37, 46–47, 49, 53, 61,
63, 98, 120, 122, 128
straight, 22
stream, 85
street, 31, 33, 59–60, 73, 75, 84, 165, 175
streetlights, 175
stress, 64, 93, 101, 113
strict, 55
strictly, 118
strike, 83–84

strikers, 83–84
striking, 30, 83
string, 95
Stripes, 68
stripped, 93
strive, 88, 150
structure, 19, 43, 46–47, 51, 53, 79, 100,
111, 114, 127–128, 136
structured, 52, 88, 104, 110, 184, 186
struggle, 77, 84, 110, 114
struggling, 64
student, 17–18, 21, 64, 85–86, 97, 143
studied, 21, 23
studio, 148, 158, 186
Studs, 32–33
study, 22, 24, 56, 74, 91, 94–95, 173
studying, 22
sturdy, 179
sub, 60, 96
subjective, 29, 40, 44–48, 53, 56, 67, 120,
124, 131, 159, 176
subjectively, 31
subjectivity, 38, 44, 47–48, 56
substantiation, 103
substituted, 190
subtitles, 193
subtitling, 56
subway, 79
succinct, 73
succinctly, 133
Sukiyabashi, 79

summary, 133
Sunday, 68, 85–86
sunlight, 175
Sunrise, 31–32
Superman, 76
Supersize Me, 123
supervisor, 144, 147–148, 155, 157, 164, 183, 194
supplement, 141
supplemental, 175, 178
supplemented, 32
supplying, 148
support, 29, 32, 42, 64, 71, 75–76, 83, 87, 90, 109, 114–115, 128, 131, 155–156, 183
supported, 20, 86, 90, 121
supporter, 71
supporting, 64, 84
supportive, 104, 156
surgeon, 94
surgical, 96
surgically, 96
surrounding, 36, 41, 62, 88, 117
surrounds, 50
surveys, 118
survival, 37, 45, 48, 77, 106
survive, 24, 37, 43, 78
Susan, 111
sushi, 79
suspect, 101
suspend, 41
Svetlana, 87
sympathy, 52, 70
symphonic, 58

Symphony, 58
sync, 176
syndrome, 101, 105
synergistic, 27
synopsis, 148
System, 111, 142

T

tactic, 77
tactile, 160
taint, 55
tale, 114, 128
talent, 21, 24, 27, 33, 79, 110, 145, 151, 158, 165, 186
Taliban, 40
tangible, 160
taped, 90
tapes, 59
Tata, 110
Taxi, 66
taxpayers, 87
teachers, 105, 113, 143
teaches, 81, 107
teaching, 17–18
team, 27, 52, 69, 95, 97–98, 147, 156
technical, 63, 69, 173, 194
technically, 117, 119
technician, 148
technique, 51, 64, 100, 117, 129
technology, 47, 99
telephoto, 163, 167
television, 19, 22, 26, 28, 47, 78, 90–91, 117, 123, 131, 146–147, 151, 159–

161, 172–174
Templeton, 60
tempting, 74
tenant, 42, 90
Tenants, 90
Tennessee, 97
tension, 89, 128
Terkel, 32–33
test, 45, 56, 87, 193–195
testifying, 101
testing, 118
texture, 35, 117, 159, 173
Thanksgiving, 28, 117
theater, 49, 55, 114, 118, 146, 160–161, 180
theatrical, 19–20, 23, 28, 49, 58, 93, 119,
121, 135–136, 143, 146, 161, 164, 166,
172, 195
theatrically, 111, 123, 146
theme, 33–34, 62, 64, 71–74, 77, 79, 87,
100, 105–106, 128, 187, 192
Themes, 71
Theoretically, 156
theorize, 45
theory, 18, 20, 106, 121, 131
Thierry, 59–60
Thom, 105
Thomas, 61, 143
thug, 83
thumb, rule of, 70, 115, 142
Tiananmen, 31–32
Tim, 36, 40–41
Titicut, 93

title, 53, 64, 150
titled, 31
tittles, 30
Tokyo, 79
Tom, 104–105
tone, 31, 88, 150, 158, 189–190
tool, 53, 80, 174
topic, 39, 42, 103, 108–109, 122, 128–129,
131, 152, 192
Toshiro, 43
track, 67, 74, 92, 115, 123, 149, 151, 159,
188–190, 194–195
tracking, 115, 181
trademark, 142
tradition, 57, 75, 80, 117
traditional, 25, 28, 50, 55, 60, 65, 86, 103,
119–120, 122–123, 150–151
traffic, 34, 195
tragedy, 87, 101
trailer, 124, 134, 195–196
train, 39–40, 45, 53, 113
trained, 55, 113
trainer, 113
training, 24, 26, 38, 60, 90, 97, 113–114,
118, 147, 151
traitor, 52
transcendence, 75
transcends, 62, 66, 72, 107
transcribe, 186
transcribed, 32–33
transcript, 193
transcriptions, 186–187

transfer, 146, 161
transform, 70, 81
transition, 117, 180, 195
translating, 186
travel, 47, 54, 77, 99, 112, 122, 151, 153
treatment, 26–27, 76, 111, 132–134, 152, 187, 196
trenches, 41
trends, 60, 106
tribalism, 48, 92
tribe, 48
Trilogy, 102–103
tripod, 159, 165
trolled, 131
trouble, 42
troubled, 85
trust, 107
trusted, 188
truth, 18, 25, 28, 38, 43–44, 58, 75, 88, 100
tungsten, 175, 177
tungsten balanced, 177
turntables, 63
tutors, 97
Tutu, 105
TV, 19, 161, 172, 174–175
tweaking, 189, 194
twins, 96
typical, 32, 57, 69

U

ugly, 87
UMW, 83
undefeated, 52, 97–98
underdog, 52
underground, 82
unedited, 34
union, 83
unit, 102, 149, 151, 158, 174, 178
universal, 94, 107, 128
universality, 30
University, 17, 22–24, 85, 94
urban, 90, 98
USA, 52, 82, 84, 142
user, 161
Ushio, 63–65
Utah, 91

V

vague, 103, 134
valid, 143
validity, 100
valuable, 34, 61
value, 53, 77, 106, 116, 143
Vancouver, 52
Vandross, 111
Vega, 110
vehicles, 20, 33, 40, 121
Venice, 24
Ventura, 104
venue, 35, 67, 70, 75, 145, 157, 178, 196
Verdi, 124
verify, 44
vérité, 18, 29, 34, 40–41, 59, 84, 100, 115
Vermont, 108
version, 30, 72, 83, 106, 186, 191, 193
versus, 52, 159
vertically, 167

Vertov, 28
very, 21–23, 25, 45, 54, 61, 74, 78, 85, 92,
105, 145–146, 189
veterans, 101
victims, 101
victory, 97
video, 17, 20, 31, 33–35, 38–39, 46–47, 56,
63, 65, 74, 107, 113, 118–119, 121–122,
134, 136, 139, 141, 143, 146, 148, 157,
159, 166, 173–174, 176–177, 180,
185–186, 189, 196
Vietnam, 42, 89
viewership, 108
viewfinder, 149
village, 46
Vilmos, 67
Vincent, 108
violent, 46
violinist, 27
Virunga, 77
visible, 176
vision, 23, 27, 58, 98, 135, 147, 150, 156
visual, 39, 54–56, 58, 62–63, 73–74, 119,
141, 150, 159–160, 172, 184, 186
visualize, 28, 127, 143, 166, 181
vocalist, 110
vocational, 113
voice, 23, 26, 28, 49, 68, 72, 89, 92, 99, 110,
131, 135, 186, 189–191, 194–195
volcanoes, 123–124
Volts, 164
volume, 30, 62
VTR, 148

W

Wallace, 85–86
Walpole, 22
Walter, 86
Walther, 58
Waltz, 24, 66–67
Wang, 32
warfare, 56
Warhol, 65
warriors, 42, 52
wartime, 41
Watkins, 67
watts, 164
wealth, 105, 109
weapons, 55
Werner, 37, 58, 123
Wesley, 85
West, 46–47, 80
Western, 124
WGBH, 111
whales, 76
wheelchair, 52–53
whisperer, 107
Wieden, 62
wiki, 161
wikipedia, 161
willingness, 42
Willoughby, 110
wind, 42

Winterland, 67
wireless, 157
Wiseman, 93, 126
Witch, 102
witchcraft, 102
witness, 44, 86, 112
witnessed, 31, 39
Wolper, 23
wolves, 78
woman, 65, 75, 81, 83–84, 101–103, 110, 173
Women, 94, 102–103
worship, 102–103
woven, 28
Wrapped in Steel, 71
Wray, 68
write, 25, 40, 50, 132, 134, 136, 183, 187
writer, 23, 26, 32–33, 134, 144, 147, 151–152, 187
Wyatt, 86

Y
Yasuaki, 65
York, 30, 60, 65, 69–70, 81, 114
Yoshikazu, 80
YouTube, 34

Z
Zachary, 64
Zana, 80–82
Zeldes, 110
Zeppelin, 68
Zhou, 95

zoom, 166–167, 177
Zooming, 167
Zsigmon, 67
Zuzuki, 105
Zwerin, 69

NOTES:

Bibliography and Index

Bibliography and Index

Printed in Great Britain
by Amazon